GROUNDED

GROUNDED

A Fierce, Feminine Guide to Connecting with the Soil and Healing from the Ground Up

Erin Yu-Juin McMorrow, PhD

sounds true
BOULDER, COLORADO

Sounds True
Boulder, CO

Some names and identifying details have been changed to protect the privacy of individuals.

Published 2026

Cover, jacket, and book design by Rachael Murray

Printed in the United States of America

BK07432

Cataloging-in-Publication data for this book is available from the Library of Congress.

ISBN: 978-1-64963-440-5

eBook ISBN: 978-1-68364-613-6

FSC
www.fsc.org
MIX
Paper from responsible sources
FSC® C016245

To all the seekers, the healers, and the stewards of the land.
May our voices come together to elevate the conversation.

The author wishes to acknowledge the Traditional Custodians of the lands on which I have primarily lived and worked during the completion of this book. I acknowledge the Traditional Custodians of the land, waters, and skies on which my Melbourne area workspace is situated—the separate and distinct Dja Dja Wurrung, Taungurung, and Wurundjeri Woi Wurrung Peoples. I acknowledge the separate and distinct Eastern Maar and Wadawurrung Peoples as the Traditional Custodians of the Great Ocean Road's land, waters, and skies. I also acknowledge the separate and distinct Tongva and Chumash Peoples as the Traditional Custodians of the coastal Los Angeles Basin's land, water, and skies. I acknowledge the cultural diversity of all Aboriginal, First Nations, and Native American Peoples and honor Elders past and present. I express gratitude for the continuous living cultures, sharing of wisdom, and ongoing contributions of all Aboriginal, First Nations, and Native American Peoples.

CONTENTS

PREFACE

The original version of *Grounded* was published in March of 2021, a particularly potent time for all of humanity. We were collectively rocked by a worldwide pandemic; the shockwaves of unprecedented protests and upheavals around race and human rights; major cultural and political debates around public health, privacy, and consent; and the role of social media in the spreading of views and information. Conversations around intergenerational trauma and healing, particularly around the legacy of colonization, have moved into a more mainstream position than seen in recent history. More recently, Artificial Intelligence (AI) has entered mainstream use, with yet-unknown effects on individuals, communities, society, and institutions. Natural (and unnatural) disasters, armed conflicts, and political divisions have raged onward, and the threat of authoritarianism is on the rise globally, along with the destabilization of international agreements and markets worldwide. What we now call "the attention economy" and the role of social media in our lives and businesses continues to expand, massively affecting democracies and increasing the possibility of a global techno-dystopian future for humanity.

These experiences have inspired a fresh look at the topics and concepts covered in this book. With the grace of my publisher, Sounds True, I have revisited my work and updated my views. While much of the original text remains, I have edited significant parts (including a new introduction and updated climate data) with what I hope is a more developed, current, and mature perspective. I have most certainly grown as a person and an author in the five years between my final edits and the current time of writing, and the world continues to transform in ways that are new to humankind.

Meanwhile, the climate emergency has accelerated. At the time of editing and re-publication, about 10 years have passed since the well-known COP21 climate talks and agreements in 2015 in Paris. In 2025, the global population was at 8.2 billion and climbing (it was 8.1 in 2024). 2024 was the earth's hottest year on record, according to the National Oceanic and Atmospheric Administration (NOAA)'s National Centers for Environmental Information (NCEI).[1] In the same year, we reached a record high 422.7 average annual ppm (parts per million) of carbon in the atmosphere[2] (418.95 ppm in the previous year), far surpassing the "safe" level of 350 ppm recommended by climate scientists.[3] Global ocean heat content was the highest on record,[4] and polar sea ice was the lowest on record as of March 2025.[5] We live in unprecedented and wildly uncertain times.

More than a decade has passed since this project first sparked in me. The decades to come will inevitably unveil more of humanity's collective choices and path. Perhaps our work here is more vital than ever. The need to tend to our inner worlds, our nervous systems, and mental health has never been greater. The need to act, in big and small ways, to tend the Earth and her systems has also never been greater. And the need to nourish strong, healthy relationships and communities with reciprocal care is more important than ever. We've never had more compelling reasons to reclaim what inherently belongs to us, spiritually and internally, and allow that process to both be informed by and to flow through our relationship with the earth and each other.

While we journey through some deeply troubling and challenging topics, this book is devoted to being a balm, a safe space to reflect and to learn. We will focus on big issues, but also on small, simple steps in terms of solutions. I do prompt several optional places to stop, rest, breathe, and reset throughout the book if and when it feels appropriate to you. My desire is that this revised and updated version of *Grounded* can offer encouragement and hope, a place to connect with deep emotions when needed, and action steps to attend to your body, mind, spirit, relationships, and the earth.

INTRODUCTION

This book is about heartbreak and hope. The heartbreak of the climate emergency, biodiversity loss, desertification, and the violation of the sacred. The hope within connecting to Mother Earth, becoming resilient as individuals, communities, and societies, restoring our soils and ecosystems, creating real change, and becoming loving stewards of the land again. It's about truly reconnecting with nature at spiritual, practical, and embodied levels. About remembering our inherent interconnectedness to each other and all things. And living in a balanced way that nourishes our bodies, our communities, and our soil.

I originally thought I was writing a book about soil health and climate change, but the journey brought me to the feet of the divine metaphor: the fertile soil is feminine. All over the world, as old as time, there have been Great Mother, Mother Nature, and Great Creatrix goddess archetypes. The Mother Goddess. Pachamama. Gaia. The divine feminine. She houses the seed, life gestates in the dark, new life is born, and eventually it returns back to the Mother.

A note to the reader before moving forward: I am aware that the terms *Great Mother*, *Great Father*, *god*, and *goddess* can be triggering. Please feel free to replace these as you read with anything that feels safe and aligned to you. I also use gendered language for clarity of reading, but again, please feel free to see these as placeholders and replace any terms with whatever feels true to you. We are working with symbols, archetypes, and energies which are far more fluid than hard-and-fast.

Perhaps the Great Father, the divine masculine energy, is the great steward, protector, and guardian of the soil. He brings fertility within the seed and tends the soil with care and integrity. No matter what your spiritual or religious perspective, the feminine and masculine archetypes of the soil and the seed are age-old and undeniably powerful. These energies are not specific to gender; they are part of each of us. We are working with the dance between steady structure and fluid receiving energy; the calm protector and initiator of the masculine, and the flowing, adaptable, womb-like, creative nature of the feminine. As we find balance within ourselves, we become better able to create balance in our outer worlds.

Perhaps, when the healthy masculine and healthy feminine energies get out of balance, people and the Earth suffer together. Perhaps, when the abusive masculine (physical control, hierarchy, and domination) and the abusive feminine (manipulation, sabotage, and deceit) run amok, we create a very sick, extractive, and narcissistic society. A society that poisons its own food, water, and soil, that takes everything for the few and leaves nothing for the many. A society that steals rather than stewards, that manipulates rather than nurtures. A society that colonizes, co-opts, and violates the sacred at every turn.

The story of soil itself begs deeper questions about what is going on with us psychologically, relationally, and energetically. Many of us feel disempowered, grief-stricken, and rageful at the injustice of it all. At the gruesomeness of industrial agriculture, factory farming, genocide, authoritarianism, and war. All the while being told if we just buy more stuff and numb out, we will feel better. I believe our souls are begging to differ. We know, deep in our bones, that there is a greater calling to reconnect with nature, our own spirits, and each other. And we know, despite all the horror, that there is hope somehow.

How then, do we begin to heal from the ground up? To bring balance within our inner and outer worlds? To energetically and symbolically root into something eternal, nourishing, and stable, perhaps even magical? How do we get (and stay) grounded in unstable, uncertain, and disorienting times? I suggest that we start where we are. Start with the simples. Start with the breath, and imagine a connection to the earth, the soil, the microscopic life underfoot. Listen to the whispers of Mother Nature. Start by honoring the sacred in yourself, in the place you are, connected to the bit of earth that you inhabit in this moment. Perhaps tune into the yin element of resting and receiving. If nothing else, just breathe in and out and listen. While we absolutely need to act in many instances, acting from a grounded place is more effective than acting from a frayed nervous system, fear, or panic.

The principles of balance, harmony, reciprocity, and interconnectedness are everywhere in nature. From the microscopic to the infinite. Waking and sleeping. Night and day. Healing from the ground up invites us to learn from nature as we balance our lives, design our cities, and participate in institutions. The climate emergency clearly reflects systems that are wildly out of balance. Perhaps Earth's ecosystems are being affected by our internal energetic imbalance as individuals and collectively. If we desire to work with Mother Nature to bring these external systems back into balance, we must reach within ourselves and make changes in our relationships, our businesses, families, and societies.

While so many of our current systems, institutions, and collective ways of being exact harm on all people, all genders, all beings, there is a particular connection between honoring the feminine by empowering women and girls around the world and turning the tide on the climate emergency. Access to education and reproductive rights are at the heart of the dire situation we have collectively created. Katharine Wilkinson, formerly of Project Drawdown, highlights the role of women in food production on small plots around the world, describing how that work ties in with protection of forests, as well as how reproductive education and rights have as much (or more) of an impact on our collective climate footprint as renewable energy.[1] Wilkinson urges us to be messengers, hearts broken open, in this journey. Protecting our forests; getting into right relationship with animals, plants, and fungi; healing our food systems; and freeing and protecting women and girls from poverty, genital mutilation, sexual assault and harassment, and sex trafficking are all mission critical to creating human systems aligned with Mother Nature. There are only wildly positive effects to healing soil and supporting women and girls, and we need to do these now to turn the climate emergency around, no matter what else we do. Unequivocally. It's a no-brainer.

Healing with indigenous peoples and lands also lies at the heart of our collective story, and that which has yet to be told. The legacy of colonization, of harm to indigenous peoples and earth-based systems of spirituality all over the world, is a legacy of human life egregiously out of balance. The fact that what many now call "regenerative agriculture" (a term I do use in this book) seems to be a rediscovery of ancient and modern indigenous practices of tending the soil and biological reciprocity, is clearly worth noting. While we honor the Earth Mother, the feminine energy within ourselves, and women and girls, we can also remember the role of healthy masculine stewardship, guardianship, and care of all people. The role of tending and protecting rather than conquering. So many of our hearts and our ancestors' hearts are broken from displacement from our original homelands. So many humans over so many generations have had their relationship with their homelands, traditions, families, and communities forcibly broken under the notion of private property, colonization, and war, leaving us foundationless and sometimes feeling spiritually rudderless.

While some current spiritual traditions and forms of organized religion are places of community and connection for many, legacies of pain and abuse exist in others, leaving deep spiritual wounds over generations. Perhaps the simplicity of rooting energetically into Mother Nature and balancing the healthy feminine and masculine energies within us can offer a healing avenue open to all. While the abusive feminine and masculine rely on the energies of taking and discarding, the balance of the healthy feminine and masculine can teach us the art of mutual reciprocity. Of giving and receiving with care, integrity, and honor. Each human's connection to the earth is sacred. Our connection to the balance of things is sacred. We are sacred.

We have the opportunity, right in this moment, to start to move with the energy of balance and regeneration. Your own cells are regenerating (and the better you are taking care of your health, the more they are likely regenerating). The plant outside your window may be regenerating a new branch and some leaves. A tree or a garden may be coming back to blooming life in the spring. Food and yard scraps somewhere are magically, miraculously turning into rich compost that can feed the next garden. Somewhere, perhaps on the other side of the world, leaves are falling to begin again. The moon is waxing and waning. Every inhale and exhale represents the cycle. We are always invited to be in a healthy relationship with all that is. Perhaps it's time to shed systems and ways of being that are no longer serving us, and to take this opportunity to create institutions, homes, cities, and societies that reflect the regenerative, reciprocal nature of the earth's cycles.

Healing from the ground up means connecting with our roots, literally and figuratively, on many levels. If it feels right, drop into your breath, and imagine your feet or lower body as roots growing into the earth. Begin to feel into the root archetype, representing home, safety, security, foundation, identity, and tribe. Feel supported by the earth and move gently; there may be deep heartbreak here. Whether your connection to your family and land of origin is healthy and thriving or not, the masculine and feminine energies in nature are here to support you. Healing the root archetype within can start simply and may also require deeper psychological work or even trauma recovery with professionals over time. This can be a lifelong journey, including healing lines of intergenerational trauma. While Mother Nature can be fierce, she also has the original nurturing mother energy within her to rely upon in this process. Beginning to heal and ground within ourselves, to have the courage to face our wounds, can support us in more deeply connecting with others as well as experiencing our own lives. As we nourish within ourselves, we can bring more clarity, stability, and energy to a world that needs us. And we can begin to learn how to keep ourselves safer as we develop healthy boundaries and communication, allowing for relational, community, and even societal healing.

Understanding ourselves as a part of nature—as opposed to as separate entities who affect nature—is foundational to this process. Restoring balance to our inner and outer systems requires more than simple changes in policy and business, although these are part of the story. We are invited to step back, look deeper, and reflect upon the inherent physical and spiritual interconnectedness of all things, ourselves included. Life is a miracle. Microscopic processes inside the cells of plants convert sunlight into energy that we humans, in turn, can use. Not only use but need for survival. Pause there for a moment. Take a breath . . . wow. The only way to understand the world of the small things that make all life on Earth possible is to trace back to the first life, our friends the single-celled organisms. Microscopic life was the first on earth, and nobody knows for sure how it came to be. Our best guesses involve comets or curious vibrations in the primordial soup (so, basically, magic, god, aliens, or . . . something).

The divine mysteries (Spirit), life on Earth (body), and our evolutionary history (science) have everything to do with soil health and the climate emergency. It's all connected, and perhaps the only way to solve the problem is to take it all in, magic included. I'm not talking about the kind of delusional magical thinking we've been engaged in as a species thus far; I'm talking about real magic. Mysteries of life and creativity magic. If we follow the thread from the primordial soup and through our basic cellular evolution, we can make our way to the present-day carbon cycle and everything that's wrong with it. We can do better by healing the soil, healing ourselves, and healing our relationship with the Great Mother and all that is. The soil is alive. All of nature is connected. And we are profoundly connected to the soil and each other.

We are also invited to remember, through our strong energetic root systems, that we are inherently worthy. That we belong here as spiritual beings, simply by virtue of incarnating. No need to earn or try to prove our worth. A collective of humans with a deep sense of innate worthiness, connected with love to the earth and each other, would create a very different looking society to the one currently in existence. How much of our heartache comes from an internal place of not feeling good enough, or simply, not enough? If "not enough" sounds like a mantra of late-stage capitalism, what might a mantra of true natural abundance, "always more than enough," sound and look like in the form of an individual or society? Regeneration and abundance are possible, from an energetic as well as a practical perspective. My hope for this book is to spark a notion or a memory of what's possible. And from there, perhaps spark a conversation, as well as some actions and practices.

Small acts, like growing a little herb garden and finding out where our food comes from when we make purchasing choices (whenever possible), can help empower us in our journeys while also making life more enjoyable. Taking breaks from social media and having real conversations can help heal our minds and keep us connected to each other. Staying connected to democratic processes by remaining aware and holding elected officials accountable is essential to grounding our institutions into real-life lived in real places. Taking steps like learning about the history of indigenous peoples on the land where we live can help reconnect us with each other and create relationships of repair, reciprocity, and tending. Integrating small practices like meditation and self-inquiry can help us develop our own inner sense of peace and awareness. Strengthening our relational tools and communication skills can vastly improve the quality of our relationships and communities. Connecting with our own feminine and masculine energies, learning how to heal from the abusive masculine and feminine, and coming back into our personal power by creating healthy boundaries and becoming more discerning, can support us in becoming better stewards and nurturers. Checking in with our own integrity on all levels will help us become a healthier part of the greater fabric of interconnectedness.

Remembering that a series of empowered individual choices can weave together to create stronger communities, societies, and institutions, and can help orient us toward a healthier, more abundant world. By reconnecting and healing the soil, we honor the life within us all. From dead zones in the ocean, to clean drinking water, to the amount of nutrients in the very food we eat, to how we care for ourselves and each other, this is a perspective on the story of everything. As above, so below; the macro reflects the micro, and vice versa. If it feels right, take three breaths. Allow the skin of the old to shed away and welcome the possibility of what's to come. Perhaps we are rebirthing ourselves and midwifing a new era, a new world, a new vision. Let's walk each other into a world of possibility, balance, and integrity.

WHERE TO NOW?

There are several ways to approach this book. Reading from start to finish is certainly an option, and however you approach it, I invite you to mind your nervous system as you read. If you find yourself feeling overwhelmed, I recommend skipping to a chapter like "The Inner Work and Outer Work Are One," or "Living a Regenerative Life." You can also find Soul Soil[2] exercises throughout, often with sensory exercises and optional journal prompts. Putting the book down and going for a walk outside, drinking some lemon water if it's available, or taking a few deep, intentional breaths are also good options. Taking a nap or going to sleep for the night might also be the best choice. Please do continue to check in with your body's somatic signals as you read, like shallow/deep breathing, heart racing/calm, muscles tensed/relaxed, and adjust accordingly. Moving through this book with a friend or group might also be supportive. I suggest tackling chapter 1 and 2 while feeling strong, clear, and ready to face in. In addition, a note and *trigger warning* to the reader: parts 2 and 4 include topics of several forms of abuse and violation, including sexual abuse.

While facing the gravity of difficult information is important and avoidance is clearly detrimental in the long run, balancing joy, lightness, and rest is equally important. This book is oriented toward compassion for self and others, while remaining clear-eyed about what we are facing as a collective humanity. Sometimes it's wise to take breaks when we have been trained to push through, and space for reflection and softness may help us in our path forward. Yes, there is heartbreak, but there is also hope. And in hope, may we find our courage, togetherness, and inspired, effective action.

PART ONE

BRASS TACKS

Nobody said it would be easy.
We have serious work to do, and a lot of it.
To begin, we must focus on the basics.
In order to create the future we want,
we must first find our feet.

1

IMAGINE THE YEAR 2050

Imagine you're a thirty-year-old mom. It's 2025, and you have just given birth to a newborn baby. 2024 was the hottest year on record,[1] surpassing 2023, with 2025 data coming in fast (with potentially record-breaking numbers). According to the World Meteorological Organization (WMO), 2024 was also the first year the average global temperature exceeded 1.5 degrees Celsius above pre-industrial temperatures,[2] and the daily global average temperature reached a new record high at 17.16 degrees Celsius.[3] The ten hottest years on record all occurred in the previous decade.[4] In 2024 (as I mentioned previously), the average annual atmospheric carbon dioxide level also reached a record high, with the monthly average peaking at 426.9 in May 2024 (20 percent higher than the average in June 1990).[5] The Ocean Heat Content (OHC) and the global sea surface temperature (SST) both hit record highs in 2024,[6] and global sea ice cover reached a record low in February 2025.[7] Global drought, flood, and fire conditions have intensified.[8] In early 2025, the United States and Russia have publicly stated their shared interest in Arctic energy projects (which are affected by the changing climate) and are potentially cooperating with each other in an unprecedented geopolitical shift.[9] Long-standing global borders and agreements have been destabilized by massive political shifts, initiated particularly by the President of the United States in 2025. The pace of change is enormous. The future is wildly uncertain.

I recommend taking a moment to pause here. If you are reading this around the time of publication, these are relatively up-to-date statistics; however, these numbers and political experiences are constantly moving and changing. If you're curious, you can easily find the latest numbers and information at your exact moment in time online. If you are reading this down the line, you'll be able to see what direction we are headed in and at what speed by looking at the most recent data. For up-to-date information about the climate crisis, the regenerative movement, and modalities for getting grounded, visit erinmcmorrow.com/grounded or follow this QR code.

All this information can take a moment to digest. Whenever you are ready, we are going to walk through two different potential futures in the next few paragraphs. The first is based on projected statistics at the time of writing. In updating this book over five years, I have unfortunately found that the most recent numbers are reflecting greater acceleration than the previously projected numbers, indicating that our situation is increasingly dire. When you are ready, we will walk through the projected scenario, followed by an alternative scenario.

Whenever you feel prepared, imagine twenty-five years have passed since 2025. You are fifty-five years old, and your baby has grown into a twenty-five-year-old adult. In 2050, the earth's population has risen to over 9.7 billion people. The oceans, as projected by NOAA scientists way back in 2014, are 70 percent more corrosive than they were, but even at that time they were already dissolving the shells of small animals.[10] Climate change, as projected by the Intergovernmental Panel on Climate Change (IPCC) scientists in 2013, is now completely irreversible by humans (except by a freak technology or act of god), and is pushing average temperatures well above the 2 degrees Celsius increase scientists have warned would be catastrophic.[11] More than a quarter of land species are threatened with extinction.[12] Fifty to seven hundred million people have been forced to migrate because of land turning to desert all over the world.[13] Supplies of clean drinking water and healthy soil for food are rapidly deteriorating. Half of the earth's oxygen is at risk because of threats to microscopic life in the oceans.[14] This is what it's like in 2050. Take a deep breath. And imagine. Again, I recommend pausing here if that feels right for you. If it feels available and appropriate, notice your emotion and any sensations in your body. Journaling could be useful here, as well as deep breathing, light movement, and reflection.

Now, when you are ready, we can imagine an alternative scenario. Again, imagine 25 years have passed since 2025. In 2050, humans have found a way to build resiliency and regeneration into their communities, countries, and institutions. Regenerative agriculture techniques have been adopted across the world, on both previously industrialized large farms as well as small and medium farms. Animal welfare has been vastly improved with industrial agriculture moving towards disappearing. Fossil fuels are being actively phased out, while use of renewable energies, including wind, solar, tidal, and more, are on the rise. Democracies have been protected, strengthened, and new ones created all over the world, allowing for poverty reduction, quality healthcare access, education and nutritional access, mental health support, and gender equality and safety, along with a vast reduction in armed conflict globally. Child-rearing is protected and supported by societies all over the world and infant mortality has dropped precipitously. Political corruption has dropped, and large extractive corporations are being phased out by resilient local economies and small businesses. Indigenous rights have been restored and protected, with land being actively returned to First Nations all over the world. Trauma recovery and grief care is widely available as we learn to better care for one another. Life expectancy is extending as communities strengthen and create resilient micro ecologies and economies, restoring forests, building soil, and protecting waterways. The arts are flourishing, and cities are becoming regenerative in nature, including clean transportation and buildings, affordable housing for all (eradicating homelessness), smart energy grids, climate-appropriate building, and increased livability. And carbon is being sequestered all over the world into healthy soils in forests, grasslands, and even farmland and urban land. Pressure has been taken off the oceans to absorb carbon, and ocean life is able to sustain and thrive with heating and acidification slowing. You look at your 25-year-old and feel proud that you are part of the generation of humans who decided to turn the tide on what was otherwise becoming a doomsday horror show by coming together, organizing, demanding, envisioning, and creating a better, healthier, more loving world for our children and future generations. Perhaps take a deep breath. And imagine. Feel the possibilities in your body.

I learned about climate change (which was still called "global warming" back then) sometime in middle school (in the early 1990s). And at the time, we were taught that our grandchildren's grandchildren would have to face the problem. I remember wondering what it would be like to be part of the generation of people who would slowly come into awareness that they were it, that the future of humanity would turn on what they decided to do. I wondered how long it would take them to figure it out. Would it come slowly and creep up on them? Would they argue about it? Would people deny it? Would it fix itself before they ever got there? And how exciting it would be. And terrifying. What might it be like to be part of the most important group of people in the history of the human species? The only group to have to—and get to—consciously choose whether to survive or to perish.

IT'S TIME

It's time. Everything happened a lot more quickly than scientists back then expected it to, and it's accelerating to this day. If you expect to be alive any time in the next twenty-five years or beyond, you're it. There's no other group of people to pass this on to. We've kicked the can as far as it will go. If we want to create a world that we can keep living in, it's time, and it's us. It's time for us to see things as they are and to stop making excuses, and it's time to summon the courage to do the work that we all know we need to do. We have a shot, but the window is small and closing rapidly.

I know it's terrifying. But if we turn that response on its head, it's also unbelievably exciting. Everything we'll do in the next ten to twenty years is of lasting consequence. No group of humans has ever had such a collective responsibility, or such a collective opportunity. As I heard it said at the Paris climate talks in 2015, we need seven billion pairs of hands (now over eight billion) to do this work, to turn this ship around. It can be done, and it's going to take all of us, together.

The number one thing we need to do today, next to slowing our fossil fuel emissions to a stop, is to devote ourselves to healing soil all over the world as quickly as possible. To have a shot at slowing the effects of climate change, we must pull carbon out of the atmosphere. A lot of it belongs in the soil, where plants can make use of it, which is where we should store it. If you have no idea what I'm talking about, you have found the right book. For many reasons, this most obvious conclusion is incredibly counterintuitive for most people. In truth, it's countercultural. Here's the deal:

- There's too much carbon in the atmosphere and in the oceans for humans to fare well in the near future.
- There's a legacy load of carbon in the atmosphere, meaning that even if we were to stop all emissions 100 percent today, we would still be barreling toward a two degrees Celsius average global temperature increase and beyond. NASA calls the land and the oceans the "other half" of the carbon and climate conversation.[15]

- Soil sequesters carbon. In fact, it's a natural carbon sink. It already holds more than the atmosphere, plants, and animals combined.[16] Carbon-rich soil is good for plants and humans.

What we need is to get down to the brass tacks. In other words, we need to get back to our roots. We need to understand at the most basic level where our food comes from and how a healthy food system actually works. We must come to terms with where we are getting our water and how the water cycle actually works. And we must ask ourselves what we're going to do with the excess carbon in the atmosphere and in the oceans and deal with how the carbon cycle actually works. How are our physical bodies connected to both the Earth itself and global systems at the macro and micro levels? And how in the world do we manage our physical reality in a sane way that preserves survival and can allow for true regenerative abundance?

These are the most important questions facing humanity today, and we need a clear-eyed look at how it all works in order to figure out what to do about it. We need, more than anything, to build from the ground up and get the basics right. But first, we may very well need to take a giant step back to gain some much-needed perspective. To get clear on the basics even, it may serve us to zoom way out, and then back in.

> Only by standing in our own ground can
> we determine our future.[17]
>
> —ANODEA JUDITH

As big as the Earth may seem to us, we are in fact a whole bunch of infinitesimally small people on a tiny, finite planet. Happily, we have co-evolved with other life-forms on this planet (plant, animal, and otherwise, including the microscopic life in the soil and the oceans) to live in both symbiosis and homeostasis. In other words, in partnership and balance with all the other life-forms here.

Unfortunately, we have unwittingly disrupted critical systems, in particular the carbon and the water cycles, altering them so dramatically that it's destroying our own habitat. Because Earth's systems are so profoundly interconnected, we're looking at far more than rapid temperature change, sea level rise, and storms. As a result of ocean acidification, biodiversity loss, and desertification, we are currently facing the sixth mass extinction of species on the planet.[18] And our soil, that six-inch layer of life from which all our food comes, is turning to dust all over the world. At the same time, the human population is growing exponentially. Adding two billion people to the current population over the next thirty years is the best guess, but it could be more. The coming storms, heat waves, droughts, fires, cities under water, war, and refugees are only part of the problem. We are facing threats to our food supply, our drinking water, and even our oxygen. We've lost 40 percent of our phytoplankton since 1950; phytoplankton are the bottom of the ocean's food chain and are responsible for nearly half of the world's oxygen.[19]

In 2013, CO2 in the atmosphere reached 400 parts per million (ppm) for the first time in recorded human history;[20] in March of 2016, the average global surface temperature crossed the two-degrees-Celsius-increase threshold beyond which scientists warn of devastation for the first time in human history—a threshold we're projected to cross for good by 2036.[21] This is all happening in real time, right now. By the time you read this, most or all of this data will be outdated, because we are moving along timelines with exponential curves. That means that nothing in our past experience is comparable to what's happening now, not to mention what's about to happen in the next thirty years and beyond.

Human survival is at stake. Without question. Everyone alive today is part of the deciding generation. Take a moment to look at what's going on in the news right now and see what is actually going on in the world. It's time to put our big-kid pants on and, as Carl Sagan says, "make our stand." Welcome to the most critical set of decisions and actions humankind has ever had to make.

With more than half of the world's population in cities, urban sustainability and global sustainability are one and the same. The world's major population centers are growing to sizes and scales never seen, driven by industrialization and population growth. And the key questions to figuring out how to reimagine these cities, which are currently creaking under their own weight and bursting at every seam, have everything to do with the basic needs of humans. Everything boils down to land, water, housing, food, and basic social and economic dignity. Basic needs are simple; the related problems and solutions are complex.

As cringe-worthy as the word *sustainability* may have become, it has a functional and useful meaning. Ultimately, a sustainable system is one that can keep itself balanced in perpetuity, rather than being poised for collapse. A sustainable city is one that is built from such systems and is connected to larger systems that can hold their own. It's also a city where people can meet their basic needs of food, water, and shelter daily. The notion of a regenerative world takes this one step further. A regenerative world is not merely avoiding collapse, but is designed, like nature, to be abundant beyond our basic needs. A regenerative system includes replenishing what we take and inviting nature to blossom in her diversity, resiliency, and fertility.

The task at hand is to connect the individual to the collective in a healthy way. At a global scale, we need to look directly at the basics and create a plan of action. And we need to start doing it before we have all the information. If we wait until all the data about what's to come falls into place before we act, it will be way, way too late. We currently have more than enough information to act in a strategic manner and in an intelligent direction, and we can adjust and refine along the way.

2

THE LEGACY LOAD

This might be another moment to take some deep breaths, do some stretches, hum, go outside, or otherwise calm and center your system. When you're ready, let's take a look at the carbon cycle. The carbon cycle is currently out of whack as it relates to humans and most creatures on the earth. I mentioned the first big problem in the last chapter: the legacy load. We know that there's entirely too much carbon in the atmosphere and that we've long since blown past the "safe level" of 350 ppm.

Stopping emissions is not going to be enough. Slowing emissions is definitely not going to be enough. We must turn this ship completely around, and there's no time to half-ass it. This unpleasant information is elegantly captured in the IPCC's *Climate Change 2013* report:

> Most aspects of climate change will persist for many centuries even if emissions of CO2 are stopped. This represents a substantial multi-century climate change commitment created by past, present, and future emissions of CO2 . . . A large fraction of anthropogenic climate change resulting from CO2 emissions is irreversible on a multi-century to millennial time scale, except in the case of a large net removal of CO2 from the atmosphere over a sustained period.[1]

Translation: to get back to where we were before, we need net negative emissions. Net. Negative. We need to not only slow and stop emissions, but to draw carbon out of the air and store it in the earth. A lot of it, over a long time. In other words, we need to do all the things. All. The. Things.

We're not supposed to talk about this because it will freak people out. People might go into a freeze state (if you find yourself here, I again encourage you to take a break and do something that brings joy and calm). Either that or they'll just dismiss the data outright. It's a lot to digest. And given how terribly we've done with the information we already have about the need to reduce emissions, the concern is that people will simply shut down and do nothing (or, in fact, continue to make the situation worse). Maddeningly, anxiety has a paralyzing effect, but in practical terms we don't have time to be stuck in fear. Even if we're afraid, we need to lean into it and keep moving forward, and the only way we're actually going to be able to grapple with the problem is to get a handle on it and face it. But for many, daily life can be overwhelming enough without all this existentially disturbing information, and hope can be extremely difficult to summon, much less the energy and ability to act.

I checked in with the lead author of this section of the IPCC report, and he was actually hopeful that if we can lower emissions quickly enough, we can adapt to what's currently occurring on the planet. I hope he's right. That said, if we were to simultaneously lower emissions and move to rapidly draw down and store carbon in the soil, it would still be of tremendous benefit to our overall situation, no matter our level of success in lowering emissions. In *Drawdown: The Most Comprehensive Plan Ever Proposed to Reverse Global Warming*,[2] the Drawdown team do a wonderful job of covering what it will take to heal the soil and sequester carbon in a wide variety of ways. In worst-case scenarios, we'd at least give ourselves a little bit more time to change our systems enough to lower emissions in the face of a growing population. In more optimistic scenarios, we actually get our act together and get ourselves on a path to net negative. Whatever happens, the Earth needs to take in one large, sustained inhale. The inhale, as it happens, is the yin part of the breath. Surrendering, receiving, taking in before and after releasing. Every natural cycle, including our breath, follows this rhythm.

OCEAN ACIDIFICATION

Next to the legacy load, we face ocean acidification. The effects of the oceans absorbing more carbon than they can hold are clear. Too much carbon in the oceans causes the ocean pH to change, and our oceans are currently quickly acidifying; they are literally becoming corrosive.

And excuse my French, but it's fucking terrifying. Ocean acidification is coming at us faster and more definitively than climate change, and climate change is coming at us like the proverbial freight train.

It's worth repeating: our corrosive waters are dissolving the shells of baby animals right now. At the rate we are going, waters will be 70 percent more corrosive by 2050, and the amount of sea life with dissolving shells could triple.[3] That's just twenty-four years from the (re) publication of this book and counting. Perturbing the oceans is an altogether horrible idea. When researching this topic, I found utterly terrifying lines like this buried in academic papers:

> By process of elimination, primary causes of mass extinctions are linked in various ways to the carbon cycle in general, and ocean chemistry in particular, with clear association with atmospheric carbon dioxide levels. The prospect of ocean acidification is potentially the most serious of all predicted outcomes of anthropogenic carbon dioxide increase. This study concludes that acidification has the potential to trigger a sixth mass extinction event and to do so independently of anthropogenic extinctions that are currently taking place.[4]

In case you spaced out for a moment, I recommend you go back and read this section from the top. And then perhaps take a few deep breaths. We all know that not doing anything will almost definitely result in dire consequences, and for most of us that freaks us out a great deal. Reading about the certainty of massive disasters definitely freaks me out. When I was up in a cabin doing the first round of research on all these topics, I literally had to stop—the information was so overwhelming, it was more than I could take (and I had already been studying it for six years). It makes sense that this type of news shuts us down, and we would much rather drink a beer and watch TV than deal with it or look it squarely in the face. Our conditioned response to escapism when we feel fear is not uncommon. I get it. Sometimes I'm there.

Personally, I have found my hope in both the simplicity and complexity of life in the soil. I also believe in human ingenuity, courage, and goodness, even (and perhaps especially) in the face of abusive bad actors and seemingly dire circumstances. The hurdles are many, but perhaps it's time to be curious about an intentional and constructive way forward.

HOW DO WE TAKE ON A PROBLEM THIS BIG AND MESSY?

Nature—which includes the earth, the universe, and all of us—is big and almost endlessly complex. Its complexity is partly why the notion of environmental sustainability is so hard to nail down, define, and fully comprehend. One field that is quite good at thinking about and understanding systems, naturally, is the field of ecology. Unfortunately, in the world of experts, we have also overdeveloped our specialization muscles, and so people in different fields can have a tough time talking to each other. Even people in related subfields are not the best at understanding each other's research. So for example, microbiologists, marine biologists, agricultural soil scientists, and climate scientists are often not attending the same conferences nor reading one another's papers, and generally are not communicating with one another at all. This stymies our problem-solving abilities and keeps us in our insular silos, often scratching our heads, missing information from other fields that could be useful. While this is changing somewhat, I believe it is still an ongoing challenge in academia.

Personally, one fun aspect of this whole journey is that in relearning the basics of things like photosynthesis, the divine and the practical have finally started to come together for me. Once again, I've learned that to expand out, I must go in. The things we haven't dealt with inside manifest on the outside. When it comes to the Earth and the carbon cycle, one broken part of the system is the soil—to get it, we must look inside and unpack it. The first thing to know, in the simplest terms, is that the carbon cycle roughly includes the atmosphere, the oceans, and the soil (including the smaller category of vegetation). It's like the water cycle, in the sense that it's finite and carbon changes forms throughout the cycle. Most of us learned this in school at some point and either vaguely remember or totally forgot about it.

We hear that carbon is the building block of life, but most of us have no idea what that means. Our lack of understanding is not terribly surprising, as carbon is almost incomprehensibly small. Not stuff most of us think about every day. Carbon is one of the most basic and mundane things around, and one of the most miraculous—the stuff of charcoal was originally born from stars. And it cruises around the earth, atmosphere, and oceans, going wherever it is sent.

Right now, there is far too much carbon in the atmosphere and oceans, and not enough at all in the soil. The oceans absorb the carbon spillover from the atmosphere, which has been beneficial for a while, but by now the oceans are over-saturated. This is not good at all, because as we now know, all that extra carbon is making our oceans more acidic. That's terrifying, and again, nearly incomprehensible in terms of what the negative consequences could be for humanity. One more time: ocean acidification is at least as big of a problem as climate change, although few are talking about it in the mainstream. Clearly, to bring the carbon cycle back into balance, we urgently need to bring carbon out of the atmosphere and put it somewhere. And as the oceans and atmosphere are swamped, the place for the carbon to go is back into the soil.

3

THE STORY OF ALL THINGS

We are carbon-based life-forms and are therefore part of the carbon cycle. As such, we are connected to all other parts of the cycle: the oceans, the atmosphere, plant life, and the soil. The element carbon moves through these parts in a sort of endless loop, each aspect intricately interconnected with the others. At every point, there are tiny life-forms, microorganisms (or microbes) that help the cycle along. These beings matter a great deal; they need our help, and we need theirs.

They live in the oceans, they live in our bodies (mostly in our guts), and they live in the soils. We ourselves are made up of at least half microbe cells.[1] So, in a real sense, we are at least half microbe. Which makes sense, because microscopic life was the first life on this planet, from which all the rest evolved, and it currently represents the vast majority of all life on earth.[2] There is no "us" without microbes. Again, this is not something most of us are exactly thinking about on a standard Sunday afternoon, but doing so offers a serious shift in perspective around exactly who we are and what life on Earth is all about.

We not only evolved from these creatures, but we are in constant symbiosis with them, day in and day out. They help us with digestion and just about everything else our bodies do. Every single cell in our bodies is in relationship with microscopic life, and as if that weren't enough, these littles also help plants to grow, they produce oxygen in the oceans, and, amazingly, they help store carbon in the soil. We are life partners, functioning side by side with these little buggers in just about every way, and we have been engaged in this funny, miraculous dance with them for as long as we have existed (although they existed long before we were even a twinkle in the cosmic eye). It might actually serve us to consider ourselves their dependents, as we can't live without them for one moment, although they can get along okay without us. Regardless, our relationship to these creatures defines our existence on this planet.

But it doesn't stop there. Within every cell in our bodies, as well as the cells of every animal on the planet, live something called mitochondria—the mission-critical part of the cell that produces energy. This little organelle is most likely the ancestor of ancient bacteria. It carries a separate bacteria-like DNA, so while we need it to work for us to be human, it is decidedly not human. And in every plant cell, the energy-producing (in this case photosynthesizing) organelle is called a chloroplast. This thing also carries its own DNA and is most likely the direct ancestor of cyanobacteria, one of the first life-forms on Earth and the one probably responsible for inventing photosynthesis and literally making all other life on Earth possible.[3]

Every living cell, then, both plant and animal, is in direct relationship to the original microscopic life that made all other life possible. We are ancestors, co-creators, and life partners with bacteria.

We also can't live for a moment without the microscopic life that lives in the soil. The words *human* and *humility* derive from the Latin word *humus* and the Greek *hamai*, which both mean "earth" or "ground." Sadly, in spite of our profound relationship with these tiny beings, we seem to be entirely unaware of their existence, not just in our bodies but also in the soil (as well as the oceans).

We've only started to truly understand what's been going on down in the soil since the 1980s—which is remarkable, considering how important the soil is to our entire existence. While we are doing our funny dance with microbes, all the plants in the world are also doing theirs. Microbes and minerals in the soil, in partnership with sunlight and water, are the champions that make energy and nutrients (read: food) available to our bodies, among many other miraculous things. In forgetting about these tiny ones, we have managed to unwittingly enact a substantial deal of damage to ourselves and to the systems of our planet.

Indeed, we have been killing this small life in the soil for quite some time, ever since we began tilling the land. By tilling the land, leaving it bare, and using pesticides on it, we've been wreaking havoc on the otherwise lively community below. This is unfortunate for everyone involved, as these little life-forms are responsible for bringing minerals to plant roots (which in turn bring minerals into our bodies) and cleansing and making space for water in the soil. They are also responsible for bringing carbon down through plants to be stored in the soil, forming stable, carbon-rich humus and healthy topsoil.

As it turns out, our killing of this underground community has likely led to the destruction of over 55 billion tons of topsoil each year by agriculture as well as the release of a huge amount of soil carbon into the atmosphere.[4] According to the IPCC, soil degradation and human land use have contributed to the release of substantial amounts of carbon from the soil into the atmosphere over the last 200 years.[5] This massacre also causes runoff, desertification (rich land turning to desert—think the Dust Bowl in America and Canada in the 1930s), and biodiversity loss, to name a few of the ill effects of our hapless doings.

Again, we are all connected. We must stop killing these small creatures and start repopulating them. Back to the brass tacks; we've managed to upend the system, and the place to start healing it is in the soil. Once we can accept that our planet is finite, we can also realize that Mother Nature is infinitely abundant if we work with her instead of against her.

The good news, of course, is that once we understand a little about life in the soil, we can help repopulate it. And thank goodness, helping it repopulate is not terribly difficult, particularly compared to other ideas about how to get carbon back into the ground. Of course, human-made sequestration projects are important and are coming along; however, nothing compares in elegance to what the plants and soil can naturally do.[6]

Not only does storing carbon in the soil help sort out the atmosphere and the oceans, but it's also actually good for the soil. Healthy soil is rich in carbon and microbial life, which means food full of nutrients, which in turn supports a diverse array of other life-forms in addition to purifying and storing water. For just about every reason, healing life in the soil is an overwhelmingly positive thing. And since there is no downside to healing the soil, we ought to (and need to) heal as much soil as quickly as possible and in every way possible, all over the world. And that means repopulating microbial life in the soil, which is relatively affordable and manageable, especially when you consider the destruction we are otherwise facing.

To get from where we are to where we want to go, we need to get crystal clear on this. Imagine looking down at your bare feet and seeing there a bunch of dark, rich, healthy soil, full of microscopic life. This is where the story begins. If you're looking for Spirit, sometimes it can help to look down.

Now, imagine microscopic life in the soil as the bottom of the food chain. Killing the bottom of the food chain eventually kills everything else above. We're not only doing harm to the place from which we come, we're destroying our partners in life—not a pretty sight for us, or for any of the other beings on this planet. So, the main thing we need to do is to stop killing these little life-forms and actually start helping them instead.

In doing their little soil dance, microbes essentially barter carbon for minerals and nutrients with plant roots. This results in healthier plants and healthier soil. Microbes are the middlemen. Voilà! When the system is working, this is what we want: nutrients up, carbon down. The soil loves carbon. It needs carbon. Imagine, in a way, that plants eat sunshine and poop carbon, and soil eats carbon. A tad oversimplified, but you get the picture. From the original primordial soup, this dance has been worked out and perfected over millennia. It's the dance of all life on Earth, imperceptible to the human eye, and absolutely mission critical.

The fact that this isn't common knowledge is frankly a little bit nuts. We unwittingly kill the stuff that makes the system work and then spend money to replace what we've lost with synthetic replacements that don't work anywhere near as well. All the while, by disrupting the smaller system, we are of course disrupting the larger systems.

Stop and breathe it in for a moment: photosynthesis is truly mind-blowing. Magical green things called chloroplasts inside of plant cells turn the sun's radiation into chemical energy. And if that isn't wondrous enough, this process splits the carbon dioxide and water the plant has taken in, creates sugars for the plant, and releases the oxygen back into the air.

The way plants sequester carbon, weirdly, is through a combination of photosynthesis and microbial interactions. In a magnificent exchange, the plant brings in carbon dioxide from the air and turns it into organic carbon in a form that is usable and delicious to microorganisms in the soil.[7] While some of the carbon stays in the plant body for energy, some gets "bartered" through the plant roots via a special fungus that partners up with the roots (called mycorrhizal fungi). This carbon can be used by microbes or can stay stably stored deep in the ground in the form of stable organic matter, such as humus.[8]

Silently, and without any fanfare, plants and microbes are doing more work and moving more carbon than all of humanity, day in and day out.[9] This is the miraculous, infinite dance of nature and the gift of the Great Mother Nature. As Paul Stamets says, "[The mycelium network] is the foundation of the food web. It holds all life together. Yet these vast underground networks, which can achieve the largest masses of any organism in the world and can cover thousands of acres, hide in plain sight; silent but sentient and always working tirelessly to create the soils that sustain life."[10]

In fact, in comparison to this marvelous, perfect process, our tube-sucking-carbon-from-power-plant-pipes schemes appear rather awkward. While there is a role for human-made sequestration,[11] it's worth noting that every plant is already a perfect "machine" fit to do the job. *Sequester* is a funny word. It means to hide away, to make separate, or to isolate. We humans have invested billions of dollars in human-made carbon sequestration, yet at the same time, plants are silently chugging along in the overlooked yet insanely miraculous act of photosynthesis. And when microbes are thriving in the soil and working in symbiosis with the plants, they're pulling carbon into the soil. One more time: plants pull carbon out of the atmosphere and deposit it into the soil (for free) when microscopic life thrives there. It's the way the system is already designed.

Overall, we would be wise to direct our attention to the places where soil is not already healthy. The basic way we restore life in the soil is by repopulating the microbial life that has been destroyed, which repairs the linkages and restores the natural symbiotic systems that automatically pull carbon in from the atmosphere and store it in the soil. It's not effing rocket science. In fact, it's incredibly simple.

There's a Chinese saying, xiao bing li da gong, which means "small soldier who does extraordinary things." Our microbial friends may be small, but they are indeed mighty.

> It is a natural human impulse to think of
> evolution as a long chain of improvements,
> of a never-ending advance towards
> largeness and complexity—in a word,
> towards us. We flatter ourselves.[12]
>
> —BILL BRYSON

In honor of the small and mighty, may I introduce the main microbe that works with plants to pull carbon into the ground: mycorrhizal fungi, which attach to the roots of plants and symbiotically work with 80 percent of them.[13] These humble mycorrhiza are perhaps the most important living organisms on Earth that few people have ever heard of. They work with both the plant and the soil microbes to facilitate an ongoing exchange of nutrients and minerals, water, and carbon, as well as help to fix nitrogen in the soil.

Tragically, we've unwittingly managed to kill significant amounts of mycorrhizal fungi all over the world. Again, however important we may think we are, we actually live in a world determined by the very small. Matt Ridley, author of *Genome*, writes:

> The pope notwithstanding, the human species is by no means the pinnacle of evolution. Evolution has no pinnacle and there is no such thing as evolutionary progress. Natural selection is simply the process by which life-forms change to suit the myriad opportunities afforded by the physical environment and by other life-forms. The black-smoker bacterium, living in a sulphurous vent on the floor of the Atlantic Ocean and descended from a stock of bacteria that parted company with our ancestors soon after Luca's day, is arguably more highly evolved than a bank clerk, at least at the genetic level. Given that it has a shorter generation time, it has had more time to perfect its genes.[14]

If mycorrhizal fungi could talk (and use limbs), they would likely smack themselves in the foreheads and ask what in the world is the matter with us. Never mind biting the hand that feeds us—we are literally killing the thing that possesses the hand to feed us (okay, they don't have hands, but you get the picture). As an example of the greatness of small things, I love that a microscopic fellow called the water bear (technically, the tardigrade) exists. It requires an electron microscope to photograph. Water bears can live in the vacuum of space, at extreme pressures, in intense heat and cold, under ionizing radiation, and without food or water for at least ten years. I introduce this fascinating creature in the hopes that you will Wikipedia them and become as obsessed as I have (and to point out just how weird and diverse life on Earth really is). Just because life is tiny, doesn't mean it can't be effing cool.

To review, we are not nearly as important as we think we are, and in a bit of hubris, we are somehow managing to kill our little partners in crime below the soil line. Again, the main culprits are the ways we have exposed the soil through tilling (in addition to poor livestock management), not using compost and cover crops to replenish and protect the soil, and employing pesticides and other harmful chemicals. The basic concept behind maintaining and supporting soil life is to replicate nature's processes as closely as possible. This means keeping the soil relatively covered and undisturbed, and relying on compost, cover crops, and other beneficial crops to protect the soil and keep it replenished with nutrients. This form of practice is generally referred to as regenerative agriculture.

Here's a checklist for not killing our beloved soil microbe buddies:

1. Create compost (let organic waste decompose rather than throwing it in the trash)
2. Use that compost instead of industrial fertilizers and pesticides
3. Avoid turning or tilling the soil and use cover crops
4. Amend the soil with microbes

Of course, there are different methods of composting and all sorts of details that have to do with what type of soil you are working with in the first place, but these are the relevant basics across the board. Again, not rocket science. Stu Campbell's book *Let It Rot! The Gardener's Guide to Composting* is a good starting place for step one. The best way to work with the soil wherever you are is to meet with garden shop owners; experienced gardeners; people who practice regenerative, biodynamic, and permaculture farming; and mushroom enthusiasts. This is important, because soil varies widely from region to region (even within microregions), and we must educate ourselves instead of relying on convenient one-size-fits-all solutions. With the basics in place, the personal education and trial-and-error nature of learning to work with a specific parcel of earth is a significant part of the fun. And knowing that we're contributing to the greater good while fostering life through love and attention is its own reward.

BENEFITS OF HEALTHY SOIL

Healing the soil is already a no-brainer decision, but it also generates many incredible side benefits, including cleaning and storing water, increasing the nutrition in plants, restoring soil structure, counteracting runoff and desertification, and increasing biodiversity.[15] Because this is how the system originally worked, restoring life to the soil essentially puts the system back into balance, and thus heals every other related system. The carbon cycle, the water cycle, and the food web are all intimately interconnected. This should come as no surprise, once we've come to terms with the interconnectedness of all things. Mother Nature is diverse, resilient, and infinitely abundant, and working with her creates a virtuous circle of positive feedback loops. The miracle and beauty of the life-death-rebirth cycle healing begets more healing. And as we turn our intention and actions towards healing, Spirit picks us up and carries us most of the way. We must only show up to do our parts, as does every other aspect of nature.

When soil microbes are healthy and doing their thing, plants get so much of what they need to be resistant to pests, obviating much of the need for pesticides. The documentary *The Biggest Little Farm*, directed by John Chester, illustrates how the cycles of life and death work together in symbiosis. Thriving microbial life also works with the plant and fixes nitrogen, potentially making commercial synthetic fertilizer unnecessary. What we have been haplessly doing instead is spraying pesticides, killing the beneficial life that helps nourish the plant, and then needing to place outside sources of nutrients into the now-dead soil. A bit silly, of course, and rather expensive. The obvious alternative is, of course, to sequester carbon in the soil. Wherever there is healthy soil, this process is free and is already taking place. Gaia in her perfection. In sum, healing microbial life in the soil:

- Sequesters carbon from the atmosphere
- Ensures plants get the nutrients they need, making food more nutritious and obviating the use of pesticides and herbicides
- Helps the soil clean and store water, creating more clean drinking water and stopping runoff (which ends dead zones in the ocean)
- Improves soil structure, counteracting desertification
- Provides more healthy soil for increased food production with less water
- Encourages biodiversity and resiliency, meaning more species of both plants and animals can rely on the soil

There are only positive outcomes from healing the soil, and not many excuses to do otherwise.

DISCOVERING THE DEPTHS OF THE SOIL

Brilliant, right? The natural world is magical. And when feeling overwhelmed, connecting with the nature outdoors and/or the nature within can be a calming and inspiring place to return to. We can feel grounded in terms of our internal energy and clarity, and we can also ground our experiences in the observable world. Microscopic life may seem invisible, but it's actually just very tiny in relationship to us. As overwhelming as life can be, I find it both encouraging and comforting to remember that all of life is one, and that we are inherently connected to all that is.

And there are practical ways, small and large, to contribute to a healthier, more resilient planet through healing the soil.

I personally didn't really discover the magic of the soil until after I graduated from my doctoral program. What struck me as incredibly strange at that juncture was how I had studied urban sustainability in a multidisciplinary fashion for six years and had barely heard about the soil or its role in the carbon cycle. I actually stumbled across the information through a volunteer group in my community at the time, which has grown into the nonprofit organization now called Kiss the Ground (I stood in as the first executive director[16] in the very earliest days of the group in 2013). In an inspiring twist, the regenerative agriculture movement has made great strides in entering the climate conversation in the last decade, and now shows up in university courses, programs,[17] and student research.[18] But I was baffled at the time that such a powerful and simple part of the climate conversation would be left out of the academic conversation. Something big seemed to be missing. And even once the story of soil entered my awareness, something even bigger seemed to be missing.

While I began the process of writing about the carbon cycle and microbes with a narrow lens, something quite a bit larger than myself began to call me. A whisper as gentle as the yin, the divine feminine. And then, of course, the divine masculine. For me, a feeling of connection to some sort of Source energy, apart from any set ideology, organized religion, or set of beliefs passed along by someone else. Something beyond the literal, physical interconnectedness of all things. A force of nature that transcends the intellectual and brings a quiet hope amidst the despair that the climate emergency can bring.

In inquiring about the climate emergency beyond my education, I discovered the soil. In inquiring about my own personal burnout post-PhD, I discovered the yin. And somewhere in the middle of all that, I discovered that the soil is perhaps the oldest divine feminine metaphor of all time. Somehow seemingly forgotten, but perhaps part of the deeper mystery of our spiritual connection to the earth. My ongoing inquiry continues: How in the world have we found ourselves as a collective humanity, teetering on the edge of extinction in a manner that feels like a runaway train?

SOUL SOIL EXERCISES

Find a quiet place in nature to place your feet on the earth. This can be right outside your door, or if you are in a city, perhaps find a nearby park. If this is impossible, place your feet anywhere and simply imagine dark, rich soil beneath them.

- Spend at least five minutes meditating on the interconnectedness of all things. What visuals and sensations come to mind? When you are done, freewrite for five to ten minutes. What wants to come through?

- Does anything come up in the form of resistance to the idea of being an interconnected part of nature? Are there any specific feelings in your body or thoughts in your mind related to this? Journal for at least five minutes about this.

- Looking around at your life, name at least three examples of the interconnectedness of all things. Where does interconnectedness show up in your day-to-day—for example, in the food you purchase and the water you drink? Where does it come from? What is the source?

PART TWO

WE HAVE HAD ENOUGH

Whatever that thing is
where birth comes screaming into life
and death exhales into eternity,
we draw from that knowing and that power.
We will not let our home burn.
Not on our watch.

4

HOW DID WE GET HERE?

How is it that we have collectively forgotten about the interconnectedness of all things, big and small? About our role in the great cyclical dance of nature and life? How has our hubris taken over so completely that we seem to believe we can take anything we want from the earth and not participate in reciprocity and renewal? How have we arrived at a place where we have largely forgotten about the sacred feminine nature of the soil, its essential role in all ecological functions, and therefore human life on earth? Is there something beyond the raw science and policy around climate change that tugs at our souls? If all of life is interconnected, how have we become so devastatingly disconnected? And why do we seem to be so abusive as a collective to nature, ourselves, and each other?

We know that dealing with the natural world the way we are now is not serving us. We're wrecking the planet.

And many of us worry that we have missed our chance to do something about it. Is it too late and is it even worth trying? Dropping into the realities of the climate emergency can bring immense sadness, despair, pessimism, hopelessness, heartbreak, and grief. It's admittedly depressing and scary, hence the seeming un-sexiness of the topic. But perhaps there's something magical in the hope that lies within the soil. Something we've collectively forgotten that brings a challenge and an invitation. Something beautiful beyond imagination.

I personally believe in prayer and miracles, as well as taking concrete actions toward solutions. I believe there is a pathway to healing from the ground up, with each other and with the earth. On our way there, it might be wise to inquire about how we have found ourselves in this predicament, staring out into a wildly unknown and potentially terrifying future. Perhaps we have some things to get curious and inquire about within ourselves and our human systems. Perhaps it's time to be with our heartbreak, confusion, fear, rage, and grief around our role in destroying our own home as a collective. Perhaps there are elements of both innocence and insidiousness in human life that inform this destructive behavior.

I believe that at the heart of us, we feel deep grief about our abusive nature with Mother Earth, about the abject violation of the sacred that is occurring every day. I have spent years studying and reflecting upon where we might have gone wrong as a collective. What is driving this madness? I've had many ideas and followed many threads, about the spiritual notion of the ego, about patriarchy, and even long-lost archetypes of goddess history. I've wondered about how our spiritual connection with the earth weaves through our relationship with science, policy, and action (or inaction). I've reflected upon the history of private property, human beliefs about the validity of owning land, animals, and people.

All these threads return me to the experience of heartbreak and hope. An immense grief about something lost or broken, perhaps changed forever. And a gentle hope that we can mend and heal, within ourselves and through our relationships with each other and all that is. But before we can work to repair, we must face and feel the ruptures that have occurred and continue to occur.

RUPTURE AND REPAIR

A primary rupture that continues to call out for attention is the energy of *taking* within humans, which does not seem to be reflected in the cyclical nature of all things. It obviously shows up in our taking more than can be sustained from our forests, our oceans, and our soils. It also shows up in abusive human relationships, where taking from others energetically, physically, and psychologically has tragically become a norm. The energy of taking or stealing, rather than receiving something given, seems to mark so much of today's collective and human experience. We've somehow created a society that makes it difficult to move through the world and manage to not be taken advantage of without becoming takers ourselves. When our major systems and institutions rely on this violating energy, and even support it psychologically, it can be an immense struggle to try to break free as individuals.

Parallel to the rupture of taking is the rupture of waste. Our mentality of discarding without care, integrity, or honor does not exist outside of human behavior. In nature, all participates, all comes from and returns to the cycle. That which is born, one day will pass and decompose back to become something new again. In this energy of waste, people, plants, animals, and all that comes from the earth becomes discardable. Disposable. Taking and wasting are violations of the sacred.

How do we repair? What's missing from these cycles of abusive destruction is the energy of reciprocity. Here we find the healthy masculine energy of giving and guardianship, and the healthy feminine energy of receiving and nurturing. The masculine plants the seed and tends to the soil; the feminine receives the seed and nourishes it through the dark, mysteriously creative gestation process, and gives birth. The masculine and the feminine hold the roots and the plant together in a divine balance as it matures, perhaps goes to seed itself, and one day decomposes back into the soil. The gendered sexual and relational metaphor is obvious, but again, these energies are not gendered. Giving and receiving with integrity exist *energetically* within us all. Fierce, gentle, and badass all at once.

The simplicity of the healthy feminine and masculine energetic balance in nature is almost shockingly elegant. But the fog of the toxic and abusive feminine and masculine in our minds, lives, and society keeps many of us in a sort of exasperating amnesia. Perhaps we have an opportunity to see what is right in front of us and connect to it. Simple, but not easy. Simple to say, but perhaps not as straightforward to do.

Healing from the ground up challenges us to look under the hood and get honest about where the abusive feminine and masculine show up in our lives. Within ourselves and our communities. To uncover the places of trauma and rupture that require tending and repair. And to begin to take the small steps, starting where we are, to come back to the home within ourselves so we can stand in right, reciprocal, honorable relationship in integrity with all that is.

If it feels right, stop and breathe. Imagine dropping roots into the ground and being held by the great biome of all of life in her diversity, including the insects, the plants, the fungi, the soils, and the trees. Feel how held you are by the Mother. Imagine dropping any thoughts that do not serve, including judgment and criticism, into the earth to be composted. Stay connected with your breath and feel into your body. Find your feet. Feel your heart. Breathe deeply.

We have much to face, and much to restore. The good news is that when we heal something within ourselves, we heal the lines for eternity from the past, in the present, and into the future. When we choose to stop lines of trauma within ourselves, we transmute the pain that has been passed down unconsciously from parents and society to children, into love. And when we share this loving work with our children and others, it ripples into the future. Perhaps this is the invitation of our time.

INHERENT BALANCE

Revolutionizing our relationship to the soil and healing from the ground up invites us to get curious about something beyond the sheer science of soil health and to connect in a soulful way with all of nature. Perhaps it's our soul—our highest self—that knows our infinite nature, transcends space and time, and wants us to expand, create, connect, and be love. Perhaps our soul is the part of us that innately knows and has always understood how nature (which is us) and the universe (also us) really work, and what is needed to keep the entire system and ourselves in balance. What if our soul is a piece of the benevolent, alive, co-creative universe expressed? Maybe, because the universe is made of love, so are we. This could be why true self-love might be a pathway to feeling grounded, integrated, and fully alive in our bodies.

Many ancient systems of knowledge and wisdom passed down to us over thousands of years in some way offer these insights, but this understanding has always been available to explore within ourselves. The wisdom of our bodies and our souls is infinite, and it's always available. We need only to tune in, listen, and drop into our bodily sensations and inner knowing. Learning to do that and to begin to trust in our personal knowing can be an entry point to the art of inner work and healing work.

Our own heartbeat is the drumbeat.

Here, we return to an understanding of the inherent balance available within us. The culture of taking and stealing can seemingly blind us to our place in the interconnectedness of all things. To our role in stewardship and nurturing, giving and receiving. To our reciprocal relationship with the microscopic and infinite. Perhaps our souls are connected to something greater and are crying out for change as we experience the heartbreak of what's before us.

This may be a good place to pause, before we shift gears into some emotional realms of pain and difficulty. A relationship with something greater than ourselves can bring great comfort and relief, and at the same time can begin to gently re-sensitize us and point us toward what is hurting. While there may be great hope, many of us still feel immense pain. If it feels right to you, whenever you may be ready, take a few deep breaths and drop into your body. Be with whatever comes up about the heartbreak of disconnection and the abuse of Mother Nature. Just take a safe moment (or longer) to feel any emotions around the devastating loss of biodiversity and harm to all beings on this planet. If you feel safe to be with fear and anger, allow those to move through. Drop into your sense of integrity and responsibility for the generations to come. Stay here for as long as it feels true to you before moving into the next chapter, which explores some of the energetic nature of abuse.

5

THE CRY OF THE GREAT MOTHER

There is an aching scream from the center of the universe. Against abuse of all kinds. The abuse that poisons our soils, waters, air, food, our bodies and minds. Against the toxic, extractive nature of taking and wasting. Against entitlement toward that which does not belong to us. Against the disregard for Mother Nature and the ongoing violation of the sacred. The scream from within me says, *This will not stand. This will not stand. Not on my fucking watch.*

For all the newborns arriving today. For all who came before and who will follow. For those who will become the mothers and fathers of the future. Humanity is not going down on our watch.

Not. On. My. Watch.

We have had enough. Force, coercion, and manipulation are unacceptable violations of the sacred. As the mothers and fathers of this planet, our duty is to protect the sacred, to say no to those seeking to destroy it, and to say yes to all the things we are growing from, learning, and creating through transmuting and alchemizing the pain. To protect the sick, elderly, young, disabled, poor, and disadvantaged. To care for the animal, plant, and fungi kingdoms, and all the earth's interrelated systems. To end sexual assault, harassment, and trafficking. To end psychological, emotional, verbal, financial, and physical abuse. To stand for future generations. To heal the lasting wounds of indigenous cultures and lands with all people. To stand, for now and eternity, for the highest good of all. With kindness, humility, grace, and love.

Nature teaches us the inherent balance and interconnectedness of all things. It's time for us to remember. It's time for us to fully open our eyes to the forces destroying our home and everything we hold dear. Our minds and spirits have been manipulated at large scale for a very long time. Many of us have deep spiritual wounds and confusion that leave us seeking to reconnect to some kind of Source energy, whatever our spiritual background and upbringing. What can make this even harder is that these wounds can leave us vulnerable to even further abuse, as the toxic feminine and masculine have a parasitic nature that scans for existing vulnerabilities to take advantage of. Social media and search engine algorithms can fuel and exacerbate these vulnerabilities, leading to confusion and tribalism. Individuals and groups can use cult tactics and dark psychology to feed off a wounded desire for healthy spirituality. But our spiritual connection to the earth is our birthright. Our connection to our own power—our center, our rootedness and sense of worthiness—belong to us, and healing within ourselves can help us repair these torn threads. Our connections with each other in healthy relationships can be fortified to protect ourselves and our communities.

Perhaps something lies in the mysteries of Mother Nature—the experience and the archetype—that can support us feeling our way through this devastating sense of loss and betrayal. Maybe there are clues in the energetic balance of nature that can help us connect in our hearts and deeper psyches to what can be repaired and renewed. Maybe there is something older than Western science and the application of the intellect to assist us in untangling ourselves from the egregious maze of self-annihilation that the climate emergency represents. Perhaps there is some hope in the mystical, the magical, the invisible, the infinite.

GREAT MOTHER AND THE INVITATION OF OUR TIME

Many creation stories around the world started with the Great Mother—Shakti (India), Kokyangwuti (the spider grandmother of the Hopi), Ataensic (Huron), Houtu (China), Inanna (Sumer), Ishtar (Babylon), Hathor (Egypt), Isis (Egypt), Aditi (India), Papatuanuku (Maori), Asherah (Canaan), Astarte (Syria), Gaia (Greece), Demeter (Greece), Aphrodite (Assyria, Greece), and Pachamama (Andes), to name a few. The Great Mother in all her forms oversees and embodies life, magic, fertility, agriculture, birth, death, love, beauty, sexuality, war, women, pleasure, desire, passion, nature, and the earth. Goddess archetypes are nonlinear, some springing from older versions, some holding space for new ones. Mother Nature, or the Earth Mother, is just one part of this greater constellation of symbols. The Great Mother (including the dark goddess archetype) has been worshiped worldwide as the primordial cosmic universal energy, the creator and destroyer of life, goddess of birth and death, overseer of fertility of the soil. Life and death came from and returned to the soil through food and our bodies. As it happens, the Latin root word for *matter* means "mother." Look closely at an image of the Virgin of Guadalupe. You might notice a beautiful yonic symbol (a vagina) staring back at you. The. Great. Mother. The "vagin" Mary. Hidden in plain sight. Just like the soil.

This may be a good place to begin to explore the many facets of the archetypal healthy feminine energy. She is the fertile soil. She welcomes the seed, envelops its gestation, and holds holy space for birth. Life springs forth from her and she nourishes its roots. She lives in constant exchange with all that is. And when we sleep, when we pass, when we cross over, she welcomes us back. She oversees the transition. She is the great inhale. She is the garden. She is the Great Mother. The yin.

And she is holding us gently in facing our shame, grief, disconnection, fear, and rage, welcoming us back in our darkest hour. To face her is to face ourselves. To humbly face our own darkness, our own suppression, our own shadow and confusion. Our own fragmentation and denial. Our own sacred sexuality, our own death, our own voice, our own freedom, our own power. She is our pleasure, ecstasy, grief, and rage all at once. She invites us to remember our inherent value and our power as embodied parts of the living, ever-unfolding universe. Sacred geometry spills from her skirt folds. She is nature herself, and she whispers to us that we are part of her. That we have always known. That we have everything we could possibly need. That she is infinitely abundant and we are forever safe when we walk with her.

She is gentle and fierce. Creative gestation is both powerfully ferocious and incredibly patient, with impeccable boundaries. She allows for space to rest, in order to receive. She represents her own form of the healthy *no. Unacceptable. Not another step forward without serious consequences.* She disallows abuse, toxicity, and spiritual violation. And she longs to heal with the healthy masculine energy, the Great Father.

This is he who tends, protects, and stewards with great honor and integrity. Who is also responsible for fertility through the seed and works with Mother Nature in the miracle of creation. He also represents a healthy *yes*, a healthy drive forward, and knows how to take a stand and to defend the sacred when necessary. He reconnects us to our vision and our purpose and can take the lead. He can be a passionate, bright light, while also being gentle enough to tend to the vulnerable.

Together, the healthy feminine and masculine energies within us are co-creative forces of nature. Together, they dance in infinite cycles of beauty. They honor and set permissions and boundaries. They remind us of our inherent worthiness, our sacredness, and our responsibility to tend to all of creation. They remind us of our integrity, our value, and the art of reciprocity. They teach us when we falter and represent a coherent whole that is ever in motion, and still always in balance. And they have zero tolerance for that which seeks to take, extract, steal, abuse, or behave in an entitled way.

As we remember the healthy feminine and masculine, we remember their role in nature's fertility and abundance. I'm always blown away by the number of seeds that plants produce. Each basil plant, for example, produces hundreds when it goes to seed. It only needs one to replace itself, yet it produces more than enough for a person to save for years and years' worth of basil plants. Magical. And the seeds that don't become new plants or get collected for the future return to the earth and go back into the cycle: nothing wasted. What is meant to germinate and grow will grow, and all else will be returned to the cycle. Profound abundance. I'm pretty sure the goddess is hiding in your compost heap. The secret is in the perfect design of things as they work together.

While these energies are, again, ungendered, there is a metaphorical relationship between the healthy, fertile soil and the womb. Women—the cycles of our bodies, of menstruation and childbirth and life and death (for all of us who do and do not bleed)—are intimately tied to the cycles of nature, of the seasons, the moon, and harvest. When we do not let the soil rest, we tear at the connective fabric of the earth to take more than she is ready to give. When, societally, we do not support parents in the process of childbearing and child-rearing, we drive humans to exhaustively extract from ourselves just to make it through a day. When we allow toxicity and abuse to be embedded in our institutions and organizations, and we do not identify these things at the individual level in a way that protects ourselves and others, we participate in a system of ongoing extraction and co-optation. Perhaps restoring the balance between the healthy feminine and masculine energies requires us to firmly identify the toxic human versions of each.

The toxic feminine energy relies heavily on social, emotional, and psychological manipulation and coercion, to maintain and control social status, steal creative work, and take credit for that which does not belong to her. She copies, co-opts, spreads rumors, threatens, sabotages, lies, counterfeits, and runs smear campaigns. She fakes true relationships and connections. She misdirects, shifts blame, and takes zero true responsibility for her actions. She has no creative juice of her own, in stark contrast to the healthy feminine.

The toxic masculine maintains a false hierarchy and authority, mainly with physical and verbal force. He uses violence and the threat of violence to steal and exert a false ownership over people, animals, and land. He bullies, trespasses, intimidates, and physically harms the innocent. He plunders rather than protecting. He destroys rather than stewarding. He has no integrity and no sense of responsibility.

Both the toxic feminine and masculine carry the energy and illusion of entitlement to all forms of creative life force that do not belong to them. Both violate. They feed on energy that they have no right to. They exercise energetic, psychological, emotional, physical, and spiritual rape. Rather than honor the beautiful reciprocity of all things, they take, steal, copy, extract, plunder, and destroy all that is sacred, all that is holy. And unmasking how these toxic energies operate lies at the heart of disarming them—in every person and system on this planet, including within ourselves.

Abusers, of course, come in all forms and gender identifications. They show up in all sectors and industries. As do victims of abuse. Perhaps this energetic conversation is particularly important because both the toxic feminine and the toxic masculine energies run rampant on this planet at the time of writing. Learning to identify these forms of abuse where they exist can support us in healing from the ground up. Much heartbreak lies in this area of inquiry, and our collective trauma lies deeply at the heart of what we now consider the climate emergency. Full-scale trauma recovery is the topic of many other books, but beginning to discern and to also look inward is a significant starting place.

The topic of discernment could also fill another volume, but working with healthy boundaries is a good place to start (I explore this in chapter 12). Sometimes we need to drop into the center of grief and rage to really feel them. While we are often encouraged to disconnect from our anger, it can be an excellent alert system when violation is occurring. It can mean that a boundary has been crossed, a *no* has been ignored. Connecting with healthy, righteous anger can support us building a practice of discernment within ourselves, helping us to identify where these toxic energies may exist.

Another form of discernment is feeling into your body's more subtle signals about a person or system. This can take some practice, as many of us have a sense of numbness, dissociation, or even confused signals after living our lives inside of unhealthy systems. But we can notice feeling drained before, during, or after interacting with someone. We can feel mined for information, time, attention, or money. And we can practice feeling into whether a person brings a truly supportive presence, or one that actually feels like control. A sense of self-abandonment or contorting, dissociating or sometimes leaving the body, can also alert us to a toxic presence or pattern. Feeling smaller somehow, in the short term or over time, can also be a flag that somebody is mining or extracting from us, or cutting us down, even subtly. Ongoing confusion, brain fog, the bait-and-switch of intermittent rewards can signal that someone is consciously or unconsciously manipulating us for their own gain. Simply feeling drained, stressed, or violated during or after interacting with someone can signal that something needs attention in a relationship.

Real work with the nervous system can help us understand triggers, and working with an excellent mental health practitioner can be of great support. One therapeutic approach, Eye Movement Desensitization and Reprocessing (EMDR), can be extremely supportive for healing through traumatic events, and Richard C. Schwartz's Internal Family Systems (IFS)[1] method can also be very effective. Learning about trauma and the body can take on many forms and can be paired with self-study around various methods of discernment. Of course, discernment is equally necessary in identifying genuine skill and a great match in choosing a practitioner to work with. Unfortunately, not all practitioners are created equal, and training, certifications, or degrees do not always equal integrity. I recommend deeply vetting any care practitioners, and making sure that they are a good match for you and your needs.

With the proper support, applying these methods and practices to our relationships can support us in choosing and nurturing great, healthy, reciprocal relationships, while letting toxic ones go (and staying out of them in the first place). Healthy, thriving, safe relationships are the social "healthy soil" where the individual can truly blossom and express as their whole self. If more people exercised these practices in their social lives and in the workplace, there would be considerably less tolerance for the abuse that arises from the toxic feminine and masculine at the individual and societal levels.

I make no illusion that this work is easy, but the toxic feminine and masculine show up in the obviously devastating forms of human extraction like mining and deforestation, all the way to the subtle realities of bad actors inside nonprofit organizations with a mission to help heal the earth. Overfishing, pollution of all kinds, and poisoning our own soils are simple illustrations of this toxicity at work. False gurus, co-opted leadership, corruption in all sectors, and stealing from indigenous cultures represent more complex examples. Conversely, the archetypes of the healthy feminine and masculine energies can help us envision a renewed balance and ethos of honorable reciprocation in all relationships.

RECLAMATION, REDEMPTION, AND REGENERATION

Healing from the ground up invites us to right these relationships—within ourselves, with others, and with the natural world. To become loving stewards to ourselves and the land again. These toxic energies of taking and stealing, and the bizarre illusion of entitlement, stand directly against the notion that we are, in fact, a part of nature and not standing over it somehow. Perhaps there is a gentle avenue for safe spiritual inquiry, available to everyone and separate from overarching human ideologies. Perhaps there is a pathway to reclaim what is inherently ours and return to a place of wholeness within us and within the natural universe.

Let's take a moment to shake off the toxic, abusive feminine and masculine energies (we will revisit them in chapter 12) and begin to find our way back to what is possible, to what already exists within us and in nature. In the physical and the invisible. Maybe take a few breaths if that feels right. When we love our bodies, we connect to food and love the earth. When we spend time meditating on the trillions of cells that make up each of our bodies, the trillions of atoms that make up those cells, and all the spaces between, we can perhaps stop for a moment to simply be in awe of what we are made of. Perhaps when we connect and turn inward, we can unpack the mysteries of being and living.

This is not just woo. It's a perspective based on empirical evidence. Practical and mystical all at once. Here's a simple truth: all life is one. Here's a simple possibility: we take ourselves way too seriously. Maybe if we could just stand down for a moment and breathe it in, we could see what's right in front of our faces. We are soil. Soil is life. Maybe we can't see the forest for the trees. As we are unconsciously thrashing about our lives, many of us seem to be starting to get the sense that there may be a greater truth out there. Reaching this place of possibility may invite us to slow down, get quiet, and take a giant step back. Perhaps we have been standing on the truth all along. What if the simplest solution on the planet is beneath our feet? Wouldn't that be a trip? Some part of us may resist the idea that it could be that simple, but what if it were? Perhaps we can open ourselves to the notion that this world is not always what it seems, and that our illusions and blind spots could be—literally and figuratively—the root of our problems.

> Wherever you go in the world, whatever
> animal, plant, blob you look at, if it is alive,
> it will use the same dictionary and know
> the same code. All life is one.[2]
>
> —MATT RIDLEY

Welcome to the "persistent flawed thought that we are separate from the world," as MIT-trained artist and scientist Jeff Lieberman puts it.[3] The separation from the earth that we perceive is utter nonsense. Just nonsense. Lieberman recommends that we see the entire world as our own body. If we could see this truth more clearly, how would we behave differently? Would we feel the balance of the healthy masculine and feminine energies in our own bodies, as well as the Earth and all her creatures? Would we drop the toxicity in ourselves and seek greater integrity in all relationships? Would we shed toxic relationships and nurture healthy ones?

The healthy feminine and masculine invite us to connect with something deeper, as well as identify the places where we are out of integrity as individuals and as a collective.

There is a way forward, but there have been (and continue to be) many violations, many ruptures that have brought us to this place. The disorientation of living in this world can inspire a great deal of fear. We may feel a sense of exhaustion from it all, and perhaps an overwhelm of our systems. At the same time, there are opportunities in the challenges, and ways forward that encourage gentle restoration on many levels. Small steps can matter as much as big breakthroughs. Reciprocal care for oneself and others can be a great place to begin to check in. As we grapple with these concepts, maybe we can find some more easeful, loving balm in the wisdom of the ages.

THE GRANDMOTHERS SPEAK

Some time ago, one of my teachers introduced me to a gentle book, *A Call to Power: The Grandmothers Speak, Book 1* by Sharon McErlane.[4] Here, the (spiritual) grandmothers—elders from all traditions—guide us all back to balancing the yin on this earth. They remind us of the feminine principle, the fertile soil—how to root and how to release. The grandmothers also guide us to trust ourselves and never force ourselves (or any plant or animal) to grow too fast. To each its own pace. They return us to ceremony, play, joy, beauty, and the sacredness of all life. With kindness, patience, and humor, they remind us of our place in the fabric of being and encourage us to let go of judgment and attachment, and to perhaps pray together. They utilize the tree of life to remind us of the balance between in-breath and out-breath, receiving and giving, rooting and rising, mother and father, yin and yang. They help us feel the connection through our underground root network to all places and peoples of the earth, to each other and all life in a web of interconnectedness. We open the net of light by breathing into this web with peaceful, loving intention.

So, we breathe deeply. Drop in. Imagine the root systems beneath our feet and the connections between us all. Feel our hearts beating and the love that runs through everything. Remember, the grandmothers whisper. Living a soul-filled, love-expanding, open, empowering life of personal freedom is an every-day, every-moment embodied practice. Leaning into an economic system that provides opportunity for all to choose a life that aligns with the earth is fundamentally critical. Our choices in terms of what we eat, our relationship with the earth, what we purchase, how we travel, and how we treat others are all reflections of our inner state. We can only truly transform the world for good by transforming ourselves. Along the way, we get to dismantle what no longer serves us (or never did to begin with), as well as create the new world systems in its place.

Imagine for a moment a world society operating from a fully expressed, soul-fulfilling, love-based place. Just imagine. Breathe. Feel the resistance. Breathe again. And imagine. It's so beautiful. Love first. Hearts open. Personal expression. Balance with the earth. Abundant regeneration. Social equity. Dignity. Freedom. Music. Art. Play. Institutions that reflect our true desires. Imagine.

Let's make our way to healing from the ground up. Healing from toxicity and abuse and finding true reciprocity. Finding a balance between our own inner work and the outer work that can be done to support life on earth.

Finding a balance of the healthy feminine and masculine within ourselves and learning from Mother Nature's whispers about the cycles of the earth as we go. Let's connect to our rootedness, our inherent worthiness, our resilience, and courage. Perhaps we can learn to reclaim and own our power, feeling emboldened to lead a regenerative life. Let's find our humility and the strength to repair what has been ruptured, to grieve fully when life calls for it, and to stay curious about the journey.

SOUL SOIL EXERCISES

Find a quiet place where you can set aside between five and ten minutes. Take five deep breaths. Let yourself sit with any grief and or rage that comes up when feeling into the presence of abuse, manipulation, and toxicity. Allow anything that you might not initially want to look at or feel to come up. Journal for as long as feels good and freewrite on the following questions:

- Where do you find abuse, manipulation, and toxicity showing up in your life? What comes up when you start thinking about it?

- Find a way to physically express these feelings in private (my favorites include punching/primal screaming into a pillow in a parked car or other private space, crying, running, and dancing).

- Identify ten places in your life where you can untangle yourself from toxic, abusive, and destructive relationships. Keep your list in a journal or place where you can revisit it as a self-check-in.

- Sharing about these experiences with a trusted and qualified professional can also be supportive. Close friends and trusted community can also be supportive, but be sure to exercise great discernment in who to share with.

PART THREE

HEALING FROM THE GROUND UP

Finding our feet on the ground
and finding our energetic roots
is the first step to healing
from the ground up.

6

INNER WORK AND OUTER WORK ARE ONE

From this place of balancing the healthy feminine and masculine energies, how do we begin to reweave the interconnectedness of all things within ourselves? How do we face the challenges of our time without completely breaking down ourselves? How do we manage jobs, relationships, child-rearing, personal health, and day-to-day life inside of corrupt systems, and still somehow attempt to contribute to positive change on a regular basis? How do we manage existential dread and massive insecurity about the future inside of a cascading collective mental health crisis? We are now exposed to 24/7 images of genocide and war, spin machines, internet trolls, algorithmic mind control, crazed billionaires, ever-growing natural and unnatural disasters, and on, and on . . . How do we manage to calm down enough to rest, take a break, and even enjoy elements of life, while so many are suffering around the world? How do we grieve the already difficult parts of life, while also grieving the massive horrors around us?

I don't have one simple answer to all of this (I'm not sure anybody does), but I do believe there are a set of multifaceted approaches that can help. Most of the rest of this book is devoted to the relatively simple and the small, which I am aware are humbly nested inside a wildly complex set of societies, institutions, and rapidly changing global circumstances. Most likely we are not all going to change the entire world by taking a walk, drinking some tea, and meditating alone. But perhaps the better we can manage our nervous systems (even if just by remembering to breathe as we move through our day), the more we can protect our health, think clearly, and better care for others. Perhaps learning better relational skills can help us become and stay connected in healthy, loving community. Perhaps consciously contributing to a healthier food system that is better for the planet and her people can have small ripple effects outwardly and personally healing effects inwardly. Perhaps making one small but significant lifestyle change like composting can give us even the tiniest sense of agency and refill our wells for more challenging work. And perhaps learning from indigenous peoples and wisdom, working to repair our deeply wounded collective past, can offer some true healing and orientation in this chaos. The fact that you picked up this book and care about the climate emergency is something already.

Perhaps let your heartbreak lead you to rest, and let your hope lead you to action. Maybe the inner work and the outer work need to be in balance. I personally have found, at various points in my life and career, one group of people or another vehemently insisting that one is more important than the other. Maybe we are tired of being at odds with ourselves and each other and need to find a way to build a bridge here. I personally spent my studies and the early years of my career focused on some deeply challenging and seemingly intractable issues, including homelessness, environmental degradation, and climate change. I initially focused on policy change—imagining, hoping, and believing that this might be the best way for me to contribute to positive change in service to humans and the environment. Very long story short, I worked very hard, learned a lot, and ultimately burnt out. Burnout is only becoming more extreme as the world itself becomes more extreme, and to be fair, a big part of my personal burnout at the time was relational. Our bodies and our minds are not actually built to sustain the onslaught of digital information coming at us, compounded by our mostly sedentary work lives and other challenges. Perhaps caring for our systems and our bodies is necessary in caring for the earth.

If it feels right for you, take a moment here and find all four corners of each foot on the earth (outdoors, if possible, but anywhere will do). Take three long, deep, cleansing breaths. Scan your body for anything that does not serve you and imagine releasing it into the earth, where Mother Nature can compost it and turn it into something more useful. No matter what is going on in the outside world, we can work with our inner state. Of course, mindset work, rest, and rejuvenation must be balanced with action in the world. At the same time, burnout and freeze states can keep us from thinking clearly or acting from a centered place. As the world becomes increasingly disorienting, with a dizzying pace of change and seemingly endless crises and atrocities, we must find a way to take care of ourselves and each other. In the US, mounting economic pressures and growing wealth disparity from an increasingly extractive capitalistic system are pushing many of our lives and bodies away from rest and toward a breaking point. The *how* we take care is not always obvious or easy.

With simple grounding, breath, and mindset techniques, we can meet many things going on inside of us with love and compassion. We will explore several of these approaches in the coming chapters. Professional mental health support, healthy relationships, and strong communities are also critically important beyond individual inner work and are part of building networks of community care. "Self-care," depending on how it is approached and understood, can indeed represent avoidance or bypassing, or it can represent a necessary nervous system reset and moment for physiological repair. There's no one-size-fits-all approach to this process, but perhaps it is worth reflecting upon the human need for balance and rest in life, in a world that can push us into overdrive and overwork to the point of overwhelm, paralysis, or breakdown.

My personal journey toward balance started with a light yoga practice as well as Western therapy in my late twenties and early thirties while finishing graduate school. Yoga helped my body relax from long hours in front of a computer, and I treated it primarily as exercise and a mode of unwinding. During a particularly stressful time, my first therapist handed me a book called *Lovingkindness: The Revolutionary Art of Happiness* by Sharon Salzberg. I was immediately mesmerized—the book helped me disarm and untangle some heated social conflicts in my life right away just by managing my perspective and inner state. I employed Salzberg's meditations and mindfulness techniques to guide myself away from the world of intellectual control and to lessen my tendency to grip onto external experiences and conflicts. At the same time in yoga, I remember feeling astonished at the sense of peace and calm I experienced during Savasana each time.

Competitive athletics in high school and college had generally kept my body balanced with academic work; even so, I remember constantly feeling exhausted. Everything in my life (except for the few years I spent solo traveling) had been about excelling, pushing, achieving, and winning at something. Like so many of us, I found myself on a trajectory of achievement and productivity that seemed to be a train with no brakes. Whatever this force was, it wanted me to be well-liked (but not intimidating), to look good (within certain parameters), to be sought after sexually (but not overtly so), to marry well and bear children (at which point I would hand over my autonomy and sexuality in this particular schema), to make as much money as humanly possible with a good and respectable job title, and no matter what to have a solid 401k and an excellent image.

Essentially, it started to feel to me that my entire task in life was to avoid rejection by anybody or anything, and thus to keep my egoic sense of safety intact by maintaining an unassailable image and never take any risks. I had spent a good part of my life playing along, resisting, rebelling, running away, and otherwise reacting to this utterly unwinnable set of demands. In retrospect, I believe I was seeking healthy relational balance in life but was vastly unaware of the effects of trauma bonding, codependency, the inner critic, and a host of other unhealthy relational patterns that would take me years to discover and learn about.

Just before I turned thirty, I left a six-year relationship and devoted myself to a process of attempting to find my authentic self. Through this process of discovery, I've found layer after layer of conditioning and unhealthy relational patterns, and I've spent years exploring what feels like every modality toward my own wellness and mental health through personal and spiritual growth. Some of these modalities have been extremely helpful, many have been incomplete, and some have been frankly misguided. Importantly, throughout the process, I've learned a great deal about discerning the efficacy of certain approaches, as well as the integrity of various practitioners and "guides." This exploration has gone hand in hand with my unfolding relationship with nature, the food I eat, chosen community, and my personal creativity. Healing from the ground up can take many forms, and I realize now that for me, every intentional breath I have taken has been gently guiding me back to a sense of Spirit, back to myself, and back to Mother Nature. In yoga, for example, while I started out thinking I was relaxing and doing something that simply felt good for my body, it turns out that moving with attention to the breath can be more profound. My experience has been similar for me with gentle meditation, going to a farmer's market, or taking care of plants indoors.

Perhaps what we truly need in our personal lives is a mirror of what we need worldwide. As we create a regenerative world, we create regenerative lives for ourselves. Imagine what that might be like: taking the time and space to replenish our personal well without guilt, shame, or ridicule. Co-creating a world where we can actually slow down enough to take a breath. The human spirit, body, and mind need constant nourishment for us to create outwardly. Imagine a water well. If we take and take endlessly from that well, it will eventually dry up. We need to give it time to naturally replenish so that it can keep providing water for us. Now imagine the earth. The same concept holds true. The earth naturally replenishes and finds balance, and it's up to us to work with her and provide this space. When in balance and equilibrium, it requires little effort. The system naturally rights itself and finds alignment and balance when we only take what we need. It's the magic of Mother Nature.

Through my personal process of healing from the ground up, I've found that inner work and outer work are deeply connected and mirror each other. I've found that working with plants and the soil, beginning to heal my relationship with indigenous peoples and lands, and working to create a more just and equitable society all feel integral to the healing of my soul. For me, the modalities of yoga, meditation, breathwork, and mindset inquiry have all aided in my growth in relationships and infusing love into my life and work. As gardening teaches me patience (as I mentioned before, the grandmothers make it clear that no plant or human should ever be rushed), I've learned that fighting and controlling in the name of creating a better world have not been effective for me. Yes, the injustices are innumerable and nearly incomprehensible in their reach. Still, for me, the path requires co-creating lovingly with Mother Nature and trusting her guidance and the alignment of all things. While perhaps our minds feel certain that we must push, move, and break things with brute force, Mother Nature asks us to surrender and flow in a dance of inspired acting, releasing, and receiving. This can allow us to be replenished and ready to go when it is indeed time to act. In cooperation, we can take turns with our fellow humans.

While imperfect and easy to lose track of, practicing balance has been deeply valuable in my life and work. What has become abundantly clear to me is that the way so many of us have been taught to treat ourselves is the way we as a species have been mining the earth. Hopefully, we are currently living in the last vestiges of an extractive system, both in our relationship with the earth and in our relationship to our personal well-being. What would it look like to be in balance and the flow of abundance instead of endlessly taking? What would it look like to give back?

Here's another opportunity breathe a little more deeply if that feels right and available. Perhaps there is an element to this that is not actually work. Maybe not toxically hard work, the way so many of us have been trained to believe the nature of "work" is. Facing our inner fears is real. And generally, terribly uncomfortable. At the same time, the yin is about receiving. Yes, we face the brass tacks. Yes, we go back to the basics. And at the same time, maybe Mother Nature is imploring us to receive what is already here. What always has been with us. The abundance of the Earth herself. Regeneration. What do we do in the world to create the vision we so desire? Maybe we roll up our sleeves and receive, rather than extract. Maybe we let some of the soil rest while new life prepares itself. Maybe we steward and protect rather than take and plunder.

As embodied souls, we clearly have things to do in the material world. Healing soil all over the world is no small task. At the same time, perhaps it can be joyous, especially when we have a larger perspective on what we are up to regarding human life on earth. As we remember and integrate Mother Nature, we can work with the Earth herself to create positive feedback loops that can right the system. Maybe we have what it takes to encourage virtuous rather than vicious cycles.

In terms of action, some burning questions are: What do we do, specifically? And how do we do it? My answer is as follows: we must do both the inner work and the outer work to get to where we are going. The inner work suggests going inward to inquire, get curious about, and work with the parts of ourselves that keep us locked in these hopelessly failing systems. The outer work involves building a more regenerative world in practical ways. Both are relational and involve reciprocity. In the coming chapters, we'll walk through both some inner work exercises as well as some practical steps to support regenerative political, economic, social, and ecological systems.

Without a doubt, we must heal our institutions, our notion of a healthy economy, and the intergenerational injustices wrought by toxic abuse and manipulation. As we dig in, our relationship to self-care and inner work must remain strong. Just as a well can get dried up, if we take too much from ourselves without giving ourselves time to rest and replenish, we can become martyrs instead of co-creators. Thankfully, we can remember that we are working with nature, the Great Mystery, each other, and the universe (whatever your sense of the universe is). And just as the regenerative agriculture model is all about working with nature and replenishing what we take to create more abundance, we can create regenerative lives that allow us to both give and receive in balance.

A PLACE TO START: PUT YOUR BODY ON THE EARTH

Step one: put your body on the earth. Ideally your whole body, belly to the earth, but just finding bare feet or hands on the earth is a start (once a day is ideal, if at all possible). Placing your hands in the soil to grow living beings or walking and lying on the earth for any amount of time are even better. Just to calm down, take a moment, connect with the earth. For many, of course, access to an ideal place to walk or rest is not always immediately available. Some of us live in cities with minimal park space, in cold climates, in places with spiky plants and bugs/snakes/creatures (like in the desert), etc. My personal workaround for this is touching a (non-spiky) tree or plant that has roots in the ground—or even a potted plant if that's available—and just breathing.

If you can find your way to them, I personally find forests with soft soil or beaches to be ideal (obviously use your judgment about where you are) for a lovely reset. When I have the chance to wander around barefoot over soft, rich soil, my body and entire system calm down in a way that I can't fully explain. It's like a total reset for my nervous system, body, and soul. Sleeping next to a rushing creek or a body of moving water can also be very calming and restorative—perhaps the darkness and the sound of water simulate the womb in our minds and bodies. If you can find a beach for camping—with no electrical lights or road noise, with waves as the only sound—the ocean can provide deep rest. Creating lived environments where all people have access to the natural world is part of our collective healing as well.

All this is to say that there are profoundly restorative effects of connecting with the earth directly, whenever possible. In a restless world, finding a way to connect with nature in big or small ways can support us in pulling away from screens and devices, resting our minds and our eyes, calming our nervous systems, and perhaps breathing a little more deeply. For my personal sense of well-being, connectedness to nature, and health, nothing beats lying on the earth. In grounding, we literally ground electrons in our bodies the way we ground wires and electronic devices. Most certainly, when I go too long without touching the earth directly, I can feel it in my body. But it can be easy to lose track when numbness and various dopamine hits from social media and cortisol spikes from the news, etc. become the norm. It makes sense from a practical and physical as well as spiritual and metaphysical perspective—our bodies are part of Mother Nature, materially and energetically. As part of the interconnected web of all things visible and invisible, our bodies are never separated from the soil from which we all come.

Before I do any healing work, I ground and center. To ground, I find my feet on the earth and root energetically into Mother Earth. To center, I find my central axis and imagine a bright line moving through the center of my body, out through the top of my head into the universe, and down to the center of the earth. To me, being grounded also means being grounded in truth, being present on this earth and in my body, and fully acknowledging my birthright to be here and my connection to the earth through my body in physical form on this planet. It means being energetically centered and owning my personal power. This can also be a powerful practice before entering a space, giving a presentation, doing creative work, or having a potentially challenging conversation. Perhaps being grounded is a key to abundance and the inflow and outflow of energy. For me, simply bringing attention to my breath can be a path to Spirit, a sense of expansiveness, and the cosmos. To remember the truth of my inner, authentic spirit self, literally all I need to do is remember that I'm on the earth and breathing and notice the spaces between. Intentional breathing can transform automatic forms of consciousness into awareness. Jack Kerouac captures it beautifully:

> Everything is ecstasy, inside. We just
> don't know it because of our thinking-
> minds. But in our true blissful essence of
> mind is known that everything is alright
> forever and forever and forever. Close
> your eyes, let your hands and nerve-ends

> drop, stop breathing for 3 seconds, listen to the silence inside the illusion of the world, and you will remember the lesson you forgot, which was taught in immense milky way soft cloud innumerable worlds long ago and not even at all. It is all one vast awakened thing. I call it the golden eternity. It is perfect.[1]

What if simply touching the earth and taking a few intentional breaths can remind us of the perfection of all things, perhaps even the natural perfection of our existence—even (or especially) when we might be struggling to find self-compassion and self-love? Maybe recharging our systems, taking pauses, and keeping our wells full are necessary parts of being alive, healthy, thriving, and able to take on the challenges that this moment in human life is calling upon from us? Maybe we just need a gentle reminder; something as simple as a tree or a house plant can remind us of our magnificence.

Perhaps we want something so much better than what we've been doing, and we know it. We can easily feel trapped in our off-center states—stressed out, doomscrolling, spiraling, and escaping. Maybe that's okay and very human and understandable. Much of the situation we have inherited as humanity is not particularly easy or comfortable to face. A lot of it is dark and disturbing, if we are honest. And we are tired of it. We're tired of not being able to eat food that is safe and having our lives at odds with what's good for the planet. We're tired of feeling helpless to all of it, and many of us feel tremendous guilt and shame in knowing that we're part of the problem every day. We don't know how to bring it all together—to find the harmony that our inner knowing is crying out for. But we do know that to bring life is divine. To honor death is divine. We know that, on some level, we live in a world of infinite possibilities. Perhaps there is room for self-compassion here. Nature's inherent design is to thrive, to heal, and to create. Look around outside. Nature is designed toward beauty, abundance, harmony, reciprocity, interconnectedness, and utter perfection. Maybe we can find both hope and action in the nature within us.

CALMING THE NERVOUS SYSTEM

For the body, yin energy represents rest-and-receive mode. Perhaps we and the earth are burnt out and need to restore. Our entire collective is just beginning to understand what it might mean to unwind, to let go, to receive nourishment from the earth without mining, forcing, or taking. The energy of receiving is quite different from taking. The first thing we all can do is start to calm our completely fried nervous systems. Here are some of my favorite ways:

- Breathe with intention
- Hum/chant/sing
- Walk
- Dance/jump/shake
- Connect with the outdoors

All these activities help us get into our bodies, out of our minds, and into a more connected state. While that may sound nice, it can be a real challenge to slow down. Being alone with our thoughts, emotions, and sensations can be overwhelming. For many, it takes practice. As a teacher, particularly of yin and restorative yoga, I've witnessed so many people who are crawling out of their skin with discomfort if a yoga class moves too slowly. People wonder if it's worth the money to "not get a workout." And to be fair, active movement of course can also be very good for us.

Still, our ability to let go—even for a few minutes or an hour—to release, breathe slowly, and receive restorative benefits to our bodies, can lead us on a much healthier path, and one that's more aligned with nature. Our inner voice can emerge when we quiet down and begin to move slowly and gently. To even begin to face the magnitude of the climate emergency, we must tune in to self-care. As much as this moment may seem like a fight for our lives, perhaps part of the way is counterintuitive, through the yin—through rooting down, receiving, and connecting with the divine intelligence that is guiding us.

The breath can be a connection to Spirit—both a path and a constant, built-in reminder. Intentionally slowing the breath automatically calms the nervous system. Any time we feel wound up or out of sync, we can remember to breathe. Even just a few intentional breaths can have a healing and recentering effect. Sound is also incredibly healing. We all know the pure joy we can experience by singing along with our favorite song as loud as we want, or the soothing effect of quiet music. The vibration of our own voice can heal, align, re-center, and calm our entire system. Sound healing (through listening or creating) can have profound effects on the body, mind, and spirit.

Similarly, simple walking or any kind of gentle movement outdoors can be incredibly nourishing. The recent popularity of forest bathing highlights how this ancient, simple practice can strengthen our immune systems and boost our moods.[2] It can be easy to forget to move our bodies and get outside. A previous client of mine integrated a small five-minute walk outside with binaural beats in headphones after each day at their very stressful job, when they felt like that was literally all they could make space for. They reported that the daily routine created massive positive effects on their general well-being, their calmness, and their ability to transition to more peacefully being home after work. Breathing some fresh air while moving can be a profound healing balm, and any sort of dance, jumping, and shaking can help us release embodied trauma.

My first therapist also introduced me to the book *Waking the Tiger: Healing Trauma: The Innate Capacity to Transform Overwhelming Experiences*, which opened my eyes to the incredible healing power of shaking and movement. In it, Peter Levine and Ann Frederick describe how animals freeze in near-death situations, and when they survive, they literally shake it off. We all encounter multiple traumatic events throughout our lives, even things like a near miss while driving a car. We can work with our systems on a regular basis by being in communication with our bodies, feeling in, and shaking things off the way animals do in nature.[3] Being in tune with our somatic nervous system can help us find a sense of peace and relaxation in our lives. When we find our relax-and-receive mode (the yin), our bodies and minds can be far more open to everything, including our intuition and inner truth. From that place, we can explore more layers of the energetic mapping of the human body and how they relate to our outer experience.

Here's a moment to reflect on some elements in your life, and how they might be affecting your nervous system. If it feels right, tune in to your sensory world. How visually peaceful and harmonious is your environment?

How is your audioscape? What is the ratio of electronic and mechanical noise to silence and the sounds of the outdoors and music? Notice your smellscape, too. To whatever extent they are available to you, have you tried fresh herbs, fruits, flowers, and essential oils for aromatherapy? Do you have access to fresh air? How are the taste sensations in your world? How clean is your water and how delicious is the food you eat? And how does your world physically feel? Are you using natural or synthetic fibers in your home, and are you honoring the physical elements in your life? By sticking with natural light (sunlight and fire light), natural sounds (crickets and bodies of water), natural smells (fresh plants and essential oils), natural fibers, and rich, natural tastes as much as possible, you can vastly improve the quality of your life and help calm your nervous system. Turning electronics and Wi-Fi off, going into airplane mode, and unplugging devices entirely can also provide the calm you need for sleep and rest. Of course, access and finances can be an issue here; however, small, no-cost, or low-cost improvements can often be available to start. Are there some small (or big) changes you can make to create more space for resting and receiving in your life?

SOUL SOIL EXERCISES

- Take at least ten minutes in a private, comfortable space and drop into your body and feel what's there. Feel into all sensations (pain, itching, tension, etc.) and notice any thoughts that come up. How does your nervous system feel (wired, frayed, calm)? How does your stress level feel (high, medium, low)? What does your inner monologue say? Feel into any pain you might be feeling. Without judging or attaching, breathe into these spaces and journal for at least five minutes about what comes up. When you're done, hum for at least another five minutes to release your energy further. Practice this exercise once a day for a week and see what changes.

- Lay on your back and breathe normally for at least five minutes without interruption (if possible, make yourself super comfortable with a pillow, blanket, soothing music, aromatherapy, etc.). Then take out your journal and freewrite for at least five minutes about what came up for you. How did it feel to lay down and simply breathe? If you felt resistance, what came up for you? If you felt nourished, what did you learn? Can you incorporate this into part of your daily routine? Try this both indoors and outdoors.

- Jump, dance, or shake for the length of your favorite song. How does your body feel afterwards? Is any stress or tension released? Describe the state of your nervous system and any thoughts running through your mind before and after.

- Assess your sensory world. Wherever possible take away electronic noise, car noise, artificial light, and Wi-Fi . . . even for a few minutes a day. Replace these with sounds and smells of nature, essential oils, sun, candles and fire light, natural fibers, and nourishing foods. Do this for a week and freewrite in your journal for at least five minutes a day about the changes you're making and how they feel.

7

RETURNING TO OUR ROOTS

Somehow both my yoga practice and my work on soil health curiously brought me to the symbolism of the root chakra. No matter how many unexpected twists and turns my journey takes me on, every thread I follow seems to bring me to the same place—home, within myself, into my body, to Mother Nature, to healthy, reciprocal relationships, and my connectedness mirroring the mycelial network. Through the process of reconnecting with soil, I continue to be reminded of my innate worthiness. Root chakra work is about our foundations, home, family, tribe, safety, value, and nourishment, and is a key to healing from the ground up. Much of the work we'll be discussing in this chapter has to do with root chakra healing.

As our systems and external reality shift and transform, perhaps metaphorically we are all finding our way home. To do our good work in the world, perhaps we must understand that we belong here. That our value is inherent as a living part of the universe and the great mystery. That we don't have to earn our true value outside of ourselves. That we are part of nature. Maybe we have been running on fear only because we have forgotten who we are. When we take back our power, perhaps we can take back the narrative and change the game for humanity. It's worth asking ourselves: If our money or house suddenly disappear, who are we? If our social status suddenly shifts, or a relationship or job ends, who are we? What are we staking our identity and worthiness in?

In remembering who we are and our place in the universe, we remember that our power, our value, our worthiness is our birthright. By incarnating, like every other living being, we are born whole. The creative life force of the universe flows through us and every other part of the universe. As challenging as it is, death is transformation, a changing of forms. As we remember this simple truth, perhaps humanity is passing through a collective death and rebirth. Perhaps a way forward is to remember who we are and step back into our power as sovereign beings. To come together and stubbornly challenge the systems of destruction with our hope, resilience, and love.

This may feel hard to imagine when we feel our sense of worthiness kicked by something external: a breakup, losing a job, a diminished bank account, any sense of personal embarrassment or perceived failure. Any worthiness wound can feel terribly painful. We are human, after all, and feeling connected and valued is essential to our well-being. Healing at the root level, and bringing self-compassion, self-love, and self-forgiveness back to ourselves, is critically important. No matter how disoriented we feel, this step invites us to find our feet, touch the earth, and imagine rooting down. The more we can refill our own wells this way, the more we can truly support others in their healing journeys, reminding them of their worthiness, value, and belonging.

BASIC INTRODUCTION TO THE CHAKRA SYSTEM

I knew nothing of the chakra system when I first attended yoga teacher and craniosacral therapy training back in 2014. I couldn't wrap my practical and academically trained mind around the idea of energetic spinning discs that somehow related to aspects of myself and my life, and I had even less of an idea of how to heal or align such things to improve my well-being. Now I use the chakra system as a simple and core foundation of checking in with my internal sense of balance and overall wellness. Interestingly, the chakra system has parallels in several different traditions, including Maslow's hierarchy of needs in the Western psychology paradigm.

Eastern Body, Western Mind: Psychology and the Chakra System as a Path to the Self is a beautiful primer on this topic. I return to Anodea Judith's work again and again, and portions of it take on entirely new life as my journey unfolds. I honestly have no idea how I understood life before working with the chakra system, and I'm still learning. I tend to think of the chakra system as an energetic map. We are born with this map in our bodies, and it can be interpreted as a reflection of how aligned and in tune we are with the Earth and the cosmos. As a general overview, the basic chakra system (from the Hindu tantric traditions) consists of the root, sacral, solar plexus, heart, throat, third eye, and crown chakras.

- The root chakra (Muladhara) sits at the base of the chakra system, below the base of your spine. It represents safety and security, as well physical structure, nourishment, and having basic needs met. It is associated with the earth element, masculine energy, and the color red.

- The second is our sacral chakra (Svadhisthana), which sits below the navel and stands for creativity, sexuality (reproductive or unconscious creativity), sensuality, relationships, and the emotional body. It embodies the water element and feminine energy, and is associated with the color orange.
- The third chakra is the solar plexus (Manipura), which sits below the center of the ribcage. It represents will, self-esteem, confidence, personal power, and the authentic self. It corresponds with the fire element and masculine energy, and is associated with the color yellow.
- The fourth chakra is the heart chakra (Anahata), which represents love, emotion, grief, compassion, and joy. It's associated with the air element, feminine energy, and the color green.
- The fifth chakra is the throat chakra (Visuddha), which represents truth, speaking our truth, and manifestation through vibration (conscious creativity). It embodies the element of ether and masculine energy, and is associated with the color blue.
- The sixth chakra is the third eye (Ajna), just above and in between the eyebrows. It stands for intuition, clear seeing, and imagination.

It represents light, inner sounds, and feminine energy, and is associated with the color indigo.

- The seventh chakra is the crown (Sahasrara), which sits atop the head as a thousand-petaled crown. It represents our connection to divinity, the higher self, the universe, and universal intelligence and energy. This chakra embodies the element of pure light and is associated with bright white, golden, and violet light.

As I stated, the chakra system can be interpreted like a map—an archetypal and alchemical energetic map within our bodies. The heart is where the upper three and lower three chakras meet, bridging heaven and earth along a rainbow. I believe that many people in Western societies are unfortunately disconnected from the bottom three chakras, which can leave us feeling profoundly ungrounded and insecure. Perhaps fear-based culture has been both the cause and effect of this disjuncture and disconnection from our roots, from within ourselves, and from Mother Nature.

Through this lens, perhaps we can see just how important our human connection to the earth is in terms of our personal well-being. The energetic home, root, and starting place of our systems is the basis of how we feel and how well we operate in the world. Many of us frankly often feel terrified, insecure, stuck in comparison, exhausted, overwhelmed, and completely confused as to how to make things any better. Many of us turn to Eastern or ancient healing modalities when we are at an absolute breaking point, or when Western medicine runs out of answers for us. One possibility is that there aren't enough pill-based medications in the world to handle what truly ails us. From our personal health to climate change, perhaps for quite some time we have been treating symptoms instead of systems. We have been collectively blind to the root problem within us, in front of us, and directly beneath our feet.

For so many, at the most fundamental level, we feel like we don't belong. We don't know what the hell we are doing here, and we feel afraid. We feel like we need to earn our place in a universe that in actuality has chosen us, loves us, and co-created us with a perfectly intact map of itself inside of us. Getting grounded means remembering who we are and what we are doing here. Getting oriented. It means connecting with our inherent safety and security in this world. It means connecting with our most innate knowing, the ancestral depth and love within us.

Remembering our place in the grand dance of all things—the forests, the oceans, the deserts, the flowers, and the bees. It means remembering Mother Nature and whatever Source energy, universe, or god's eternal love that you connect with. It means remembering the protective structure of the healthy divine masculine and the receptivity of the healthy divine feminine within us. Perhaps humanity's life on Earth depends at least somewhat on this remembering. If it feels good, take a deep breath and be invited to remember.

The real magic is that to keep the system in equilibrium, the plant also gives back to the system and the whole cycle goes round and round. Nature works in balance, sustainability, and regeneration through the give-and-receive exchange of all things.

Perhaps reconnecting to and rebalancing our root chakra can help us remember our worthiness, our connection to the earth, and our sense of safety within ourselves. As we call our power back from external institutions, we can work with our nervous systems to heal current and past traumas. Similar to the trauma freeze response discussed in the last section, when we undergo experiences in our lives that we don't have tools for, we can exile entire parts of ourselves until we feel rooted and calm enough to receive them again. Being triggered can throw us from our bodies and create dissociation for short or long periods of time. If we are unprepared for certain experiences, our system can put them away somewhere in our psyche, in our body, and in our field until we are ready. When our energetic system is working properly, we feel inherently safe in ourselves and can fully feel and release experiences in real time. An aligned energetic system feels strong, safely held, compassionate, and flowing with ease.

Doing our inner work in these times can mean strengthening and clearing our systems to the point where we can revisit our more difficult experiences and reintegrate them. Perhaps the world is currently in the process of a massive root chakra healing, purging, and clearing. Old belief systems about safety and security—particularly with regard to placing our power outside of ourselves in external institutions—are falling apart at every level. Getting grounded involves facing into this process, being present with it, and feeling through it—at the personal and collective levels.

SOUL SOIL EXERCISES

- Find a quiet space to sit and breathe, ideally outdoors (but indoors will also work). If possible, lay on the earth. Imagine roots unfurling from the base of your spine, navel, or any part of you that is touching the ground, and digging into dark, rich soil (even if you are inside). Now scan your body for anything that does not serve and imagine it dropping out through the roots into the earth. When you are ready, imagine yourself drawing nourishment up from the earth, through your roots, and into your body. Be with this sensation and breathe normally for as long as it feels good.

- Next, take out your journal and freewrite for at least ten minutes about your relationship with your roots, family, identity, tribe, and sense of being supported and safe. Notice what comes up and start to feel into any places that may be calling for attention and healing. Note any thought forms, emotions, or sensations that come up that feel particularly prickly or difficult (we can use these in the next section).

- Feel yourself fully supported by the earth, either sitting, standing, or lying down. Feel Mother Earth supporting your full weight and relax completely into her. Notice the sense of being completely held. Stay here for as long as feels good.

8

WE ARE INHERENTLY WORTHY

How do we get (and stay) energetically grounded in uncertain times? Because the root chakra represents our "roots" into the soil—our connection to Mother Nature—it has everything to do with our sense of security and safety. The earth literally supports our bodies: all our food, water, and shelter comes from Great Mother Earth. Often when we feel insecure and afraid, we may have an energetic imbalance in our root chakra. The connection is both physical and symbolic. Our metaphorical root connects us to nourishment and being held, which helps us understand our inherent worthiness. With a healthy root archetype, connecting into the earth, we know we belong.

Our time in the womb and as a baby also can inform the development of our root chakra. Mindset and inner child work are available in this process of healing from the ground up, where we hold our inner child safe as our higher self, communicate with them, and essentially reparent ourselves as integrated adults, welcoming exiled parts of ourselves back. We can remind these parts of ourselves that even though we didn't know it at the time, we are infinitely safe, loved, secure, and welcome, and that we belong in this benevolent universe. With great compassion, we can potentially remember and integrate fragmented and forgotten parts of ourselves.

While there are different approaches to inner child work in many schools of therapy that are beyond the scope of this book, simply beginning to hold our inner child can be available to us whenever we are ready. Also, as I mentioned before, Richard Schwartz's Internal Family Systems (IFS) is an incredible (and relatively recent) resource for exploring what he calls "parts" of ourselves, which often have different ages, roles, and concerns.[1] I highly recommend exploring his method of accessing and working with these parts. I do encourage self-study on the topic, as well as working with a qualified, integrous practitioner if inner child work feels important for you. I have personally found that working with a practitioner as well as self-practice is a good balance for me, but again, please exercise discernment in trusting this work with another individual. The following is one approach, along with a few related exercises that can support accessing and working with emotions and thoughts that feel related to the inner child, safety, and worthiness. If now is not the moment for this, please do feel free to skip this section and return whenever it feels right for you.

In a moment of contraction (pain, fear, negativity), we can access and lovingly sit with a child version of ourselves, inquire with them, and ask what they have to say. When we can tune in and feel in, sometimes we may hear the voice of the inner child say something like "I'm not good enough." And we can actually feel connected to the feelings that we may have felt as that child in real time. Having great compassion for this part/version of ourselves can take practice and can be an important way to welcome their presence and perspective.

From here, we can utilize tools like Byron Katie's The Work[2] (some of the most life-changing work I've ever done) to inquire with the thought forms that come up. In learning to identify thoughts related to emotions (which does take some practice), we can also learn to inquire with them, and in some instances, we can forgive ourselves for believing any misunderstandings about being anything other than whole and perfect in every moment. On our own or with a supportive practitioner, we can start to integrate new thoughts and consciously shift our outdated patterns through practice.

With loving attention, patience, and practice, we can choose self-compassion and even hope in every moment. Along with self-compassion, I have learned a powerful and specific self-forgiveness practice that I find incredibly supportive in working with challenging thoughts. Once you have identified and inquired around a particular thought form, say the following:

I forgive myself for believing in the
misunderstanding that [original thought form].
The truth is [whatever is true for you].[3]

This generally sounds something like, "I forgive myself for believing in the misunderstanding that I'm not good enough. The truth is I am infinitely worthy. The truth is I am a drop of the universe. The truth is I am power and love." In *The Gene Keys*, Richard Rudd describes forgiveness as a force that comes in from the future, meets the present, and heals the past.[4] In this sense, perhaps self-forgiveness can heal intergenerational lines of pain.

> To bring Muladhara to consciousness is to
> bring awareness to our roots, to uncover
> the past, to examine it, to delve into it.
> Everything that grows above branches
> out into infinity, growing more complex.
> Going down to our roots brings us into a
> singular simplicity, and anchors us into the
> commonality of the collective unconscious.
> It brings us home to earth.[5]
>
> —ANODEA JUDITH

Collectively, we are revisiting and reintegrating the wounds of our experiences over lifetimes spanning the last many thousands of years. The grief and rage from thousands of years of human atrocities and disconnection from ourselves, each other, and Mother Nature are all too real. We can feel through all these emotions, while holding ourselves safe with our remembrance of universal love and the interconnectedness of all things.

We can ask ourselves collectively what our truth is and choose how the story ends. The truth might not be pretty, or well packaged, or at all what we expect. But in every cell of our bodies there is an ancient knowing. We know the truth. We know that the design of all things is inherently perfect and interconnected. We can see how seemingly much larger cycles (like the carbon and water cycles) are tied directly into the life cycles of the small (or what we think of as the small). We can even see that small and large are one, if we only shift and widen our perspective.

We are inextricably embodied and interconnected. Food and breath are the two constant embedded reminders that we are intimately interconnected with everything around us—in perfect balance, intake, and release. There is no such thing as waste. Everything is perfectly designed to cycle back into abundance. Again, the words *human* and *humility* derive from the Latin *humus* and the Greek *hamai*, which both mean "earth" or "ground." As we rework our world, it will be born from humility rather than hubris. The solution to our most confronting problems is here and always has been. Nature is not shy about revealing her secrets. We just have to listen.

SOUL SOIL EXERCISES

- Spend a day noticing every time an unpleasant feeling comes up. Carry a small journal with you or make a quick note in your phone about the feeling and some of the surrounding circumstances.

- At the end of the day, pick one of the experiences that you noted and practice sitting with your inner child. Imagine yourself as your higher self, and tune in to the presence of the inner child. When you get there, ask the inner child what it has to say. Journal about its response until you can distill some clear thought forms like "I'll be rejected" or "I'm not good enough." Hold your inner child safe as your higher self.

- When you feel ready and open, sit with the thought and inquire about whether or not it's true (a la Byron Katie's The Work). When complete, try some of the self-forgiveness suggestions mentioned above.

9

REMEMBERING WE ARE NATURE

Growing Our Own Food

Another immediate way to begin root chakra healing—and both inner and outer work in general—is to grow our own food and compost. It's also an incredibly practical and cost-effective activity in uncertain times. In fact, growing our own food and reconnecting with Mother Nature can be an act of revolution. In a world where our systems have proven inadequate, having a direct connection to the Earth herself, along with the ability to feed ourselves, is the ultimate root chakra safety. It helps us with physical, nutritional, financial, psychological, and spiritual autonomy.

Growing our own food redirects our power back into our own field, pulls it away from highly destructive industrial agricultural systems, and counteracts the devastating effects of deforestation. Saving our seeds is a human right, and one that takes our power back from those who would try to patent nature. It's also something we can do every day for free. The current systems only stand if we continue to participate in them. At the end of the day, our food, our homes, and our bodies all come from Mother Earth, and we can realign ourselves with her.

Growing our own food can mean a tiny pot inside an apartment, a raised bed in the backyard, or a more developed garden if we have the space. An easy and fun first step is to begin to grow things that come from food scraps—carrot tops, beet tops, and lettuce all regrow themselves in just a little bit of water. All it takes is placing the pieces you cut off and putting them in water in a window container—shallow plastic take-out food containers work great and including them in your food production means reusing plastic. Garlic chives will also sprout from an individual clove, and onion chives will sprout from an onion end. Additionally, you can save all manner of vegetable scraps in the freezer and use them for vegetable broth before they're composted.

Imagine how much free value (along with considerably less food waste) these few steps can afford. Seeds can be harvested for free directly from food you've already purchased (for example, tomato and pepper seeds). And like I suggested above, you can repurpose all manner of plastic containers (and cardboard, including boxes) for planters. The only thing you need to purchase is potting soil. Also, if you have the space, making your own compost is fairly easy. Most people don't realize how much more connected and aligned with Mother Nature we can be (and for free) in just a few simple steps.

Robin Wall Kimmerer, a member of the Citizen Potawatomi Nation and a botanist, writes about how we can love a garden and it can love us back in her path-opening *Braiding Sweetgrass: Indigenous Wisdom, Scientific Knowledge, and the Teachings of Plants.* I experience my plants very much that way. The joy of cultivating and tending to little plants, interacting with them and the soil, taking only what I need for food, and thanking them can be part of every day and every meal. Imagine honoring the earth, our food, our bodies, and our spirits through love and care this way. And if you feel like you want some extra guidance before beginning, stop by your nearest nursery or talk to a friend who gardens in the area. In-person conversations are the best (and they can build supportive and healthy community as well). Get the scoop about your local plants and soil, as every area is different. Of course, there is now a lot of information online as well. Start by asking for advice, and then just dive in! Buy some organic soil, set up whatever sized garden you have the space for, or participate in your local community garden. Pick some easy plants to start with (I recommend robust herbs or cherry tomatoes) and start experimenting! Plant what you love and keep sharing information with others. Before long you'll be learning about saving seeds, how different plants respond to variations in light and moisture, and how to take the seasons into account. Over time, you'll gather all the information you need to keep moving forward. If some plants die along the way, thank them, respectfully compost them, and keep trying. You actually can't do it wrong. You might even end up howling at the moon.

For most seeds and roots, repopulating mycorrhizal fungi can be also relatively easy and affordable. It can generally be purchased inexpensively as a soil amendment and can even be purchased online. So, one first step is to stop using pesticides and herbicides that kill microbial life and make plants sick, and then to apply compost and soil amendments to repopulate life in the soil. For those of us with conventional lawns, we can also stop using industrial chemicals on our lawns, instead opting for local and drought-resistant plants. We also keep the soil covered with cover crops and compost rather than turning it or tilling it, which unfortunately exposes the microbes and sometimes breaks the tender web of mycorrhizal fungi. By protecting and amending the soil with compost and microbes, we nourish the soil and the plants to facilitate greater carbon storage in the soil. The healthier the soil and plant life, the more carbon we can sequester from the atmosphere.

Regenerating soil is an essential and relatively inexpensive way to sequester carbon, especially compared to the billions we have already spent on research involving the carbon sequestration technology still under development. Again, all forms of carbon sequestration are important regarding the climate emergency, and human-made technologies have come a long way in the last five years and will likely continue to improve. Still, repopulating soil life is a no-brainer. Take simple steps to plant food and drought-resistant plants with healthy soil, and partake in the joy, security, health, and autonomy of saving your seeds.

Living a regenerative life is about the sacred connection of all life. We are physically made of the same stuff everything else is, and we are in symbiosis with everything that lives, as well. Perhaps healing the soil is inherently divine work. With each inhale and exhale we are in constant exchange with nature—we literally exchange elements (including carbon and oxygen) with the plants around us. In a sense, there is no separation. It can be easy to forget that all life is cyclical, not linear.

With every conscious breath, we are exchanging with all that is—living and dying. Even gentle yoga and breathwork can be powerful reminders. The breath fuels every truth we speak and every song we sing. The breath is a path, our constant reminder of the divine within us. Food is another divine reminder of cycles: what we take in from the earth becomes our bodies, and what we let go of goes back to fertilize and bring forth new life. In this way, we all have built-in, constant reminders of the life-death-life cycles, and yet we still manage to constantly forget the truth of cycles and interconnection. Everything is one. It's a simple and obvious truth, but it comes forth only when we quiet down enough to listen. The earth is telling us, our bodies are telling us, and life itself is reminding us with each breath—our true nature. By losing sight of our own truth, we've lost sight of larger truths, and the consequences are painfully evident.

Our healthy relationship with the earth is not a given. Like tending a fire or tending the soil, it requires awareness, presence, and care. As someone who once had to move eight times in three years, I can personally speak to the importance of home, security, and safety. Many of us in the West tend to take having a place to call home for granted. But I've come to learn, and painfully, that home is not a given. It must be cultivated, created, and protected. Our inner worlds and our outer worlds must be cared for and nourished, and only then can they care for and nourish us. Once again, we find ourselves back to building our bridge from here to there with attention to detail, diligence, and patience.

FOOD AND NUTRIENTS

Flavor can be a telling indicator of the nutrient richness (along with freshness) in food. Not all vegetables are created equal. If you've ever eaten a fresh tomato grown in rich, healthy soil or tasted a wild strawberry straight from the earth, you may know what I mean. That pop of incredible flavor may be nature's message to our bodies that the food is nutrient-rich and good to eat. Conversely, if you've eaten a tomato from a fast-food joint or supermarket that tastes like cardboard, you may also know what I mean. That food may have traveled or been stored some time before it reaches you.

The quality of American fruits, vegetables, and food crops has concerningly declined over the last sixty years.[1] Soil health is certainly part of the equation regarding nutrient density in these foods.[2] Also, if it's not organic, your salad is more likely to have been exposed to synthetic chemical pesticides at some point. As it turns out, a healthy plant does not need any of that toxic intervention, and what we think of as pests are usually a sign of disease and illness. Going back to the cycles of things, pests are, for the most part, there to clean out the plants that aren't doing so well. If our plants are drawing pests or an invasive fungus, it may mean the plant is not getting what it needs from the soil.

Here's a different type of cycle for you: we kill the microbial life in the soil and thereby undermine the plant's ability to get the nutrients it needs. Then the plant attracts pests. To fight the pests, we spray the plant with pesticides and herbicides, which, in turn, kill more microbial life. On top of that, because we've disrupted the nutrient cycle, we add chemical fertilizers to put back the stuff that would be naturally present if only we hadn't killed off our microbial friends in the first place. Honestly, it's utter insanity. The 2023 documentary *Common Ground*, directed by Joshua Tickell and Rebecca Harrell Tickell, illustrates some of the history and background that has created this system, as well as contemporary factors holding it in place.[3]

Plants communicate with each other through the underground network of fungi and other microbes. They send signals to each other and release chemicals that indicate what is going on with them. I recommend *The Hidden Life of Trees: What They Feel, How They Communicate—Discoveries from a Secret World* by Peter Wohlleben and *Fantastic Fungi: How Mushrooms Can Heal, Shift Consciousness, and Save the Planet* by Paul Stamets and others for a thorough look at what goes on beneath our feet. When a plant is attacked by some sort of intruder, for example, it sends signals to the other plants in the system, which are then able to release chemicals to protect themselves. Plants have even been known to share their nutrients underground with other plants who are not getting enough sunlight because they are in the shade. Beautiful, profound, and totally on point. All of life is one, we are in constant exchange, and within us lies that inner knowing.

Here again, the spiritual meets the practical. Food grown in poor soil that has been sprayed with synthetic chemical pesticides will likely be of poorer quality, sickly, and devoid of what it needs, even if it makes it to our dinner table. Yuck. And the most insane part of it all is that we are undermining a system that was already designed to work! For millions of years, humans and plants and microbes and animals have co-evolved to work out a system that benefits everyone, and instead of working with that system (like the chef in Italy I'll tell you about in a bit), we decided that we could do better by taking out parts of the system and replacing them. As a result, some tomatoes taste like wet paper and our food in general—what is supposed to be our holy nourishment—makes us sick over time. The only people this broken system benefits are the owners of and investors in corporations who make synthetic chemical pesticides, fertilizers, and pharmaceuticals. All the while, we're getting sicker by the day and spending billions of dollars trying to figure out why.

Less fresh, nutritious food, by the way, affects a lot more than our health and the size of our bellies and butts. It has so much to do with how we feel and how we can show up in the world. Even when we eat vegetables (which we typically associate with being a healthy choice), we may be ingesting deprived food from an unfortunate source. Given that we are in constant exchange of our food, it should come as no surprise that what we eat affects everything in our bodies, including the microbes in our guts, which help us do what we need to do. We're still learning how eating fermented foods and other probiotics help us repopulate the microbes in our guts that we've killed off by using antibiotics. The soil microbiome is most likely the gut microbiome's nerdy cousin.

Research is pouring out all over the place that links our mistreatment of gut microbes to physical ailments such as autoimmune disorders, as well as problems with our moods and emotional states.[4] The medical establishment, which once seemed to view soil microbes as distinct from those that live in our guts, is starting to realize that the two types aren't so disconnected after all. We've already known that there are microbes in the soil that act as antidepressants when we touch them—yet another reason to garden and interact with the soil with our hands.

In some basic sense, soil is life and we are soil. What we put in our bodies matters, well beyond the physical. Without a doubt, we can do a whole lot better than we are right now. We just have to keep in mind how all of these interrelated parts play together, and understand what that means for all of us. Ultimately we'll know by the food we grow.

SOUL SOIL EXERCISES

- When you purchase your food for the week, buy at least one thing that you can eat and regrow (I recommend carrots, beets, lettuce, bok choy, garlic, or onions for beginners). If it's at all possible to purchase organic and from a farmer's market, do so (regenerative labels are also arriving to help purchasers identify food sources). For tops and lettuce bottoms, find a container in your home that you can fill with half an inch of water and place the remainder of your chosen vegetable in the water near a window. Look online for books and other resources on how to grow food from existing plants. If you are an advanced practitioner already, share this exercise with a friend and help them learn. Notice how it feels to regenerate your own food.

- Harvest seeds from something you can regrow. I recommend tomato, bell pepper, or jalapeño seeds for beginners, from which you can simply remove the seeds directly, dry them on a paper towel, and store them in a bag, plastic container, or jar. You can also go on YouTube and watch a short video about how to harvest seeds from your chosen food. When you're ready, plant as many seeds as you like in a little bit of potting soil. Save the rest in a baggie or reusable container.

Notice how it feels to interact with soil and harvest seeds for free. If you've done this type of thing for a while, share it with someone else and encourage them along the way. How does it feel to remember that your food is a living being?

- At the end of the week, take out your journal and freewrite for at least ten minutes about your experiences with seeds. How did it feel to work with nature to create your own food for free? Check in once you get some sprouts and journal for another ten minutes about the process. What feelings do the new sprouts elicit?

10

FACING DEATH AND REGENERATION

Compost and Healing with Indigenous Peoples and Lands

The flip side of growing food is composting. If sprouts are new life, compost is the death aspect of the cycle. Food waste can actually serve as nutrients for the soil and feed the next round of sprouts. Composting is a form of giving back to Mother Nature and the cycles of nourishment, and it's also a reminder that the things we think we can't use can actually be returned to the earth with care and used for something else (the material version of releasing any energy from our bodies that doesn't serve us).

Composting also heals and protects microbial life. This means taking your organic waste (fruit and vegetable cuttings, as well as yard clippings) and allowing it to decompose and become fertilizer for plants. At home, you can store organic food scraps in the freezer until your container is full and you need to transport the scraps to your nearest compost option—maybe a green bin at home that your city takes to municipal compost, a box in your backyard, or a neighborhood pile or drop-off location. Indoor electric composting bins are also now available; however, they are still quite expensive.

If you want to learn about composting, a good place to start (other than searching online) is to talk to someone who is already doing it. If you don't know anyone who is, it can be fun to get together with some friends and figure it out. If you have children, they can help as well, and you can take the opportunity to find out what's happening in your neighborhood and community at large. Spread the word about why composting is so important and educate yourself about what's happening with local policy.

Compost is a funny thing. I find that it freaks most Americans out. For Europeans and people in other parts of the world, compost is built into their urban systems as a way of life and incorporated into personal gardens. Americans tend to associate compost with trash, bugs, odors, and possibly poop.

Most of us in the US throw away our food and yard waste into the trash. From there, it travels to a landfill with all sorts of other waste (much of which should be recycled, but that's an entirely different book), and because it's not being handled properly, the whole mess emits methane and CO2 while it's rotting, which only adds to the problem of climate disruption. It's insanity. Let me be clear: food is not trash. Ever. Organic matter is an asset. Check out the incredible work of Pashon Murray and Detroit Dirt. The earth's systems are straight up designed to move everything through a closed-loop, endless, wasteless system. Our entire concept of waste is, in fact, nonsense.

It's not surprising that we are so out of tune with compost and the natural decay of organic matter. Many of us are (understandably) terrified of death. Perhaps to become more at peace with it, we must understand that when a life-form dies, it doesn't just disappear into some anesthetized other realm. It decomposes and feeds back into the material system on this earth. Of course, this is true of our bodies and those of our loved ones, and this tends to freak us out, but our human bodies are made of organic material, whether we like it or not. As far as American culture goes, we're pretty into spring and summer, babies being born, and youth culture and so on, but when it comes to darkness, introversion, winter, bugs, poop, and anything that happens underground, we cringe or avert our eyes.

To be whole, we must embrace both yin and yang; and to move with the cycles of a healthy earth, we must breathe with it. Death is humbling, and frankly, we could use quite a bit of humility right now. Perhaps it's time to stop fighting what we've always known. All that goes to say that poop is not our enemy, and that we should not throw our food scraps in the trash, but rather compost them. The notion of infinite growth in a finite system is an inherent fail. When we remember how cycles work, we remember that compost also facilitates life. Good compost is teeming with life, and all the critters that help decomposition along are drawn to the compost heap. Composting helps build humus—a key component of the healthy, nutrient-dense layer of topsoil that keeps plant life and biodiversity thriving, especially microbial life. A plant supported by a healthy soil ecosystem and a balanced surrounding ecosystem will actually have so much of what it needs to be more resilient to pests.

When I was just starting to learn about soil more than a decade ago, I found myself in an incredible garden in Italy.

It was attached to a four-star hotel, and the garden was overseen by the hotel's chef. During a tour with the chef, I asked her what she puts on her plants to keep the bugs away. At first, she didn't understand the question. I referred to sprays and pesticides, and she shook her head and said, "Oh! Nothing! We use compost!" Makes sense to me: southern Italy has some of the best soil in the world and, in turn, some of the best water. They've passed the knowledge of how to take care of the soil down through generations, and they've never stopped doing it right. If you've ever had a meal in southern Italy, much of the glory of their incredible food probably has something to do with the health of the soil and quality of the water from which it comes.

In the same way that far too many of us treat our bodies, and in the same way that our larger economy affects our bodies, we mine the soil of nutrients without replacing them. Instead of supplementing our bodies and the soil with synthetic replacements, we can approach the whole issue and give back in a healthier way. For our bodies, that means nourishment, rest, slowing down, and connecting with the earth. For our soil, that means composting and making sure the soil becomes rich with life and dark with carbon.

HEALING WITH THE EARTH: INDIGENOUS PEOPLES AND LANDS

When we develop the tools for healing and thereby heal our connection with the land, the land herself starts to share her stories; Mother Nature herself will share her song. For as long as humans have been on the earth, indigenous peoples have nurtured this relationship with the earth and held ancient wisdom for all of time. They have also been severely punished for it.

Beginning to heal the harm that has been done to indigenous peoples and their ways of knowing is intrinsic to healing our relationship with the earth. This conversation is highly sensitive and requires the utmost reverence, as it is tragically fraught with extensive violence and trauma. For nonindigenous peoples, a good place to start is looking within ourselves, at our family history and the history of the lands we live on, and to begin with questions and an open mind and heart. To inquire, be curious, and to learn.

Perhaps a more loving relationship among humans, plants, animals, food, water, and land can be restored by honoring indigenous communities and their needs, the land that bears the wounds of genocide, and the wisdom that has been carried and protected by indigenous peoples all over the world. The legacy of the MMIW epidemic (missing and murdered indigenous women and girls) is among the most tragic wounds that we collectively carry, and it requires that we awaken to the continued violence and move to end it. The horrific legacy of residential schools in Canada and the United States is also very much alive to this day (the last one in the US didn't close until 1996).

An exact way forward is unclear. However, it's obvious that we're called to honor and revere what has been harmed. All of our societies and bodies bear the cultural, psychological, and energetic scars of this terrible chapter in our collective past and present. Some initial steps[1] may include the following:

- Learn the indigenous history and name of the land you live on, and the name(s) of the indigenous people of that area.

- If possible, inquire and learn about the places where your grandmothers were born.

- Start relationships and honor them. If possible, be available to befriend an indigenous person or organization and ask how you can best help or serve.
- Learn the history of reconciliation in the region and understand what reconciliation means to the indigenous population.
- Learn about how indigenous people from your region treated the land, what was grown and eaten, and how the land was tended.
- Understand the impact colonialism had (and continues to have) on the lives of indigenous people and commit to taking steps to counter the harm.
- Discover where nonindigenous people support inequality directly or indirectly and find out what can be done to change this.
- Recognize that nonindigenous people personally are not to blame. That being said, also recognize that nonindigenous people are responsible.
- Inquire and be curious about your own ancestral wounds and connection to the land.
- Realize that much cannot be understood or experienced outside of ceremony.
- Understand the United Nations Declaration on the Rights of Indigenous Peoples (UNDRIP) and

First Nations principles of OCAP® (ownership, control, access, and possession), and why they are in place.

- Learn about key issues (for example, the MMIW and residential schooling mentioned above).
- Seek out indigenous authors and creatives to learn from.
- Improve your education by taking a course (check out ictinc.ca for options).

Actions like these can help us become aware of our painful shared reality. They can also bring to the fore the beauty of what indigenous peoples have to share and open a door for our collective healing process. Education and relationships are the keys to a way forward. Even bringing this awareness up to bear witness is a starting point, as well as a place from which to finally stop the violence still being enacted today. Perhaps here the gifts of sacred ceremony and protecting lands and waters from destruction can become woven into our hearts and societies. As we know, we are all profoundly interconnected. Harm to one is harm to all, and harm to the earth is harm to us all.

SOUL SOIL EXERCISES

- If you are not already composting, figure out the best way to compost where you are.

- If you don't have a municipal green bin or space outdoors, this means researching to find a local drop-off point. Try composting for a week! If you are already an advanced practitioner, find someone to help with their first week of composting. At the end of the week, freewrite about your experience composting for at least ten minutes. How did you feel about contributing less to landfills and giving back to Mother Earth? Are there any challenges that you have run into that can be overcome?

- Next find a quiet place and meditate for five to ten minutes on the death part of the life-death-rebirth cycle. Meditate on winter, emptying, and compost. Simply breathe normally and allow this reflection to take you wherever it does. If you feel inspired to journal, include any resistance that may have arisen.

- Research the land where you live, as well as the land one or both of your grandmothers were born on, to find out what indigenous peoples lived there. Research the history of colonialism in these areas. Freewrite for at least five minutes about what you've found and what feelings come up. Follow your intuition about what further steps to take in the list above to authentically connect with and heal with indigenous peoples and lands.

PART FOUR

INTEGRATION

Divine Feminine and Divine Masculine

All of nature is in divine harmony
in a grand dance between
feminine and masculine energies.

11

LIVING A REGENERATIVE LIFE

Perhaps the entire universe is the cosmic dance between feminine and masculine energies, and this dance plays out in each of us. Looking within can help us understand where we may have gone out of balance, as well as where we can intentionally bring ourselves back into harmony. Our personal power can be most available and alive when we honor this dance, energetic balance, and harmony.

A world in which our systems reflect this balance and are guided by divine intelligence is possible. It's a world where we are connected through our internal energetic systems and are tuned into our highest selves. Transforming our connection to the soil and healing from the ground up requires us to remember the connection between our bodies, our roots, and all of life.

We have real work to do when it comes to reversing the climate crisis. The first step is to remember who we are and where we came from. As we remember our connection to the soil and our souls, we remember our innate power, and as we do that, we can heal our energetic body systems, as well as the systems of the earth. As we remember how to connect to our inner voice and follow divine guidance, we remember that we always have absolutely everything we need. We are a part of a living, co-creative, benevolent universe. We are infinitely worthy, we belong here, and we incarnated to take on this specific task.

Now is the moment to find our feet on the earth, connect to our breath, root down, and rise. We can expand into the possibility before us when we find our roots. The magic of nature is infinite, and as it is, so are we. To find the true magic within us is to integrate the hurts of the past and the present, and to create the peaceful, abundant future we all desire. Our disconnection from our bodies and from the earth is literally killing us. The way home is back into ourselves—into our inner work—which creates our ability to express the outward solutions necessary and co-create together. Reconnecting to our true power, maintaining healthy boundaries, and communicating honestly is the way to healing our planet in time.

Humans have always understood our relationship to Mother Nature, but the times we are living in demand that we remember fully and act. The healthy sacred masculine energy holds the consistent container that allows the healthy sacred feminine energy to heal and rise again. The sacred masculine also creates the structure that allows the feminine to flow and create life, and the sacred feminine holds the holy vessel that allows the sacred masculine to show up in determined and focused action.

LIVING A REGENERATIVE LIFE: BASIC PRINCIPLES

You now understand quite a bit about the nature of the climate crisis, Mother Nature, and how we became disconnected in such a way as to lose track of the cycles of nature and our bodies. We've learned about our shared wounds and important ways to heal. The stark difference between taking a linear and extractive (mining) approach to life and committing ourselves to more regenerative practices and mindsets is also becoming bountifully clear.

What does it look like to live a regenerative life? One that is not simply sustainable (as in, not poised for inevitable breakdown), but one that actually works with the abundance of nature to create? A first step may be to set down our armor. That means relinquishing the parts of ourselves that protect the ego with cynicism, judgment, over-intellectualism, and hypercriticism. We must not allow our connection to the earth and each other to be shamed, mocked, or ridiculed; to do so is to propagate the habits of controlling others and ourselves with fear. On the pathway to joy and abundance (and our soul's expression), we often encounter walls of fear.

I offer the following as a gentle review to take step by step. Here are some simple ways to potentially live a more regenerative life:

- **Sleep.** Get plentiful, restful sleep. Simple, but not always easy. Not receiving the gift of this fundamental nourishment is a huge red flag that we are not in alignment. Western culture is famous for sleep-shaming, because it runs against the notion of endless productivity and the habit of mining ourselves in the same way we've mined the earth. Replenishing sleep is an act of revolution. Our wellness is our revolution.

We will not get run over by the bullying culture of seriousness that tries to tell us that being run ragged is strong and being well-rested is weak. When our minds spin out so completely that we can't rest well, to the point we need so much medication in order to sleep at all, something is out of line. That being said, I fully support medication when necessary. I had terrible insomnia as a teenager. I couldn't fall asleep because my mind was incessantly jumping to the next thing I needed to do to achieve, and I was constantly processing personal dramas because I had no inner compass of my own worthiness. Adequate sleep is connected to our breath and our ability to calm our nervous systems and our minds. It's also our connection to the watery, subconscious, underworld dream states, where nature and spirit speak to us. We must permit ourselves to do "nothing." There's an Italian saying, Il bel far niente, which means the "beauty of doing nothing." As it turns out, our systems are actually doing quite a bit while we are doing "nothing."

- **Food.** Obviously, this book has a lot to do with food. Eating is an act of lovemaking. How many of us have for decades been running around unconsciously or fervently shoving some food-like substance into our faces? Just to get to the next place, to do the next thing? The goddess does not shovel food. Imagine the billions of miraculous interactions in nature that result in the single apple, potato, or leaf of lettuce! The sun shining down with all its infinite love.

The poetry and flowing wisdom of the water cycle. How could we believe for a moment that the universe is not benevolent? Like sex, our relationship to food is actually about pleasure, expression, love, and the divine. When we eat, we bow to the Mother. Bury your face in some fertile soil. Be enamored with the garden. Welcome the magic of herbs and flowers. We also have a major invitation to get into right relationship with the plant, fungi, and animal kingdoms. Michael Pollan's advice in *In Defense of Food: An Eater's Manifesto* is to "Eat food. Not too much. Mostly plants."[1] That rings true. The industrial agricultural system we have been relying on for decades has been the cause of so much deforestation and soil destruction. Let's learn to take only what we need and to express gratitude for the gifts our Great Mother Nature offers us.

- **Movement.** I almost used the word *exercise* here, but movement feels more true. The body desires to move. Not simply to be "in shape," but because movement is joy. It inspires deeper breaths. It invites us into the moment. I have no idea what the science is behind dance, and I'm not sure there's an explanation. Why in the world do our bodies naturally move to some vibrations? And why does it inspire so much joy when we permit ourselves to let it rip? Why does it hurt so much when we feel suppressed in our movement? Again, feeling our bare feet on the earth is the primordial magic, the sensual language of the goddess.

- **Sex.** Amazingly, sex didn't make it to my original list. What? Blind spot. Still, our bodies desire to express themselves, and pleasure is our birthright. When we remember ourselves as part of nature, we remember that sacred sexuality is so much more than simple procreation. It's artistry and connection. It's dropping all the way in and being present with ourselves and another. This can absolutely mean self-pleasure, sensuality practices, and/or consensual partnership—or any number of nonsexual activities, like cuddling or massage. Intimacy and sex are sacred. One more time: intimacy and sex are sacred. Our creative energy is ours. We belong to ourselves and get to share this, as it serves the highest good of all. Sexual healing is real. So much damage has been enacted and passed along the lines of humanity. Some gentle, sweet, loving healing is in order. We'll revisit this topic in chapter 12.

- **Music.** Music was also not on my original list (another blind spot). Music is the voice of Spirit. Vibration is the language of the universe. I'm as far from a trained musician as perhaps anyone, but I now feel, know, and truly believe in the magic of music. The goddess speaks from the inside out. The drumbeat—pulse of our internal heartbeats—is a pathway home to the soul. However we can integrate music into our lives, the more powerful the healing we'll encounter. Music belongs to us all. Many of us have wounds here, and there are many critics and manipulators in this space, perhaps because music is so truly powerful and magical. Let's be gentle with ourselves and each other, and allow music to be the source of joy it is meant to be.

- **Giving and service.** Life is all about service. When our well is full and our cup overflows, we are able to give and serve, which is what we are actually all about. Everything in nature serves the greater good. Apparently, even the humble human appendix (mine ruptured and I had it removed as a small child), which was believed to do "nothing" for the longest time, is in fact involved in repopulating gut microbes.[2] Ha. When we give from a truly loving place, we activate our fundamental purpose—we incarnate to serve. Once we can accept our baseline safety on this earth, we have more than enough to give. Little warms the human heart as much as giving.

- **Receiving.** Again, not on my original list! The yin. And the balance to our giving. Being open to receiving is absolutely central to our wellness. And our disconnection with the goddess is the place where so many of us find ourselves disconnected from our ability to receive. Just like resting, sleeping, and eating with peace, the yin is here waiting for us to remember the art of receptivity. Our human bodies process a lot. And in order to show up for service, we must be willing to receive in balance. How deep is your in-breath? What does it feel like to be truly nourished? The story that we've been told about having to prove our worth through productivity is leaving us spiritually, physically, and psychologically malnourished. Even those of us with plenty of money. The universe desires for us to receive with joy. We meet these gifts with gratitude, and the circle continues. Feeling worthy of receiving is the challenge and the opportunity for many of us. What does it feel like to receive the gift of beautiful music? To eat wonderful food? To receive a loving touch? Receiving is essential to our humanity and our way home.

- **Nature.** We are not separate from nature. What would it be like to commune with Mother Nature on a daily basis? To nurture a plant? To pet an animal? To breathe the air and remember that we are part of it? Everything on this list is part of nature. Everyone is part of nature. Drop all the way into the earth. We are inherently safe. The only thing in the way of us receiving all of her infinite gifts is us. All we need to do is slow down. Honor earth medicine. The answer to every question, ailment, and discomfort we have is to remember. Receiving the gifts of nature can feel like punishment when we are so programmed into forcing, prodding, and pushing away that we can't remember what universal love feels like. Universal love feels like bliss. And it's our birthright. Breathe into Mother Nature herself.
- **Spirit/Reflection.** Morning and evening rituals. Checking in at least once a day with our inner nature. Perhaps you're getting the

point that all these things are the same thing. We are returning home to ourselves. And home is eternal, benevolent, ever-loving bliss. We replenish our wells by dropping in. At least once a day, remember. Just drop in, touch your heart, and choose hope over fear. Every. Single. Day. Together, this loving intention can turn the collective tide of fear into the possibility of hope.

LIVING A REGENERATIVE LIFE: PRACTICAL STEPS

Even the tiniest shifts, done daily, can change your entire life for the better. This can mean a one-minute-a-day singing practice. Committing myself to a regular meditation and writing practice has shifted my whole universe. Having a regular yoga practice has brought me more peace, health, and well-being than anything else I've ever done. Aligning with my life's purpose has brought me more joy than anything I've ever done. Finding happier, more mellow, more fulfilled spaces within ourselves also attracts like-hearted souls and helps us create a more balanced and connected outer world.

Here are five simple inner work things that you can do right now to stand in your own ground, express your creativity, and start creating our future:

- **Start a spiritual practice.** It can be yoga once a week, five-minute meditations once a day, or even reading a spiritual book. Anything that connects you with the great blessed whatever. Practicing music and creating art count, as long as you are doing them in a state of connection, rather than judgment or perfectionism. Take up or return to something that brings you true joy, whether it be painting or pottery or dance. Honor the creative life force of the universe, no matter what it looks or sounds like. Let it rip. We want to see and hear what you've got!

- **Engage in inner inquiry.** It can be therapy rooted in Western psychology, coaching, an online course, or reading a book. Again, I highly recommend the work of Byron Katie and Richard C. Schwartz. So much of what we do each day is unconscious. We need better tools to deal with our lives and deal with each other. Having better tools to deal with our emotions, our stressors, our grief, and our relationships makes life so, so much better.

- **Feel into your life's purpose, especially if you aren't 100 percent certain you are doing what you are here to do.** It's never too late or too early to find your path. Where you are is exactly perfect. Again, there are tons of resources online and in books—Julia Cameron's *The Artist's Way* is a wonderful starting point, and I also love Danielle LaPorte's *The Fire Starter Sessions* and *The Desire Map*. Joy comes from doing what you are here to do. Whatever that may be.

- **Slow down your breath.** Breathe intentionally for at least one minute a day. It's good for your nervous system. It's good for your spirit. Be in the moment. One helpful way to remember is to set alarms on your phone throughout the day. I know a startup CEO who would meditate for one minute per hour throughout the workday.

Slow it down. Inhale. Pause. Exhale. Pause. Rinse. Repeat.

- **Move your body and spend time in nature.** Place your bare feet on the earth. Go hiking. Go surfing. Do yoga outside. Walk outside. Whatever feels good to you. There's no one correct way to do it. *Earthing: The Most Important Health Discovery Ever!* by Clinton Ober, Stephen Sinatra, and Martin Zucker is a useful primer on the benefits of putting bare feet on the earth. *The Earthing Movie: The Remarkable Science of Grounding* by Rebecca and Josh Tickell is also available for free on YouTube at the time of writing. To whatever extent possible, find your way toward natural light (sunlight, candles, fire) and limit exposure to electric light. Mind your soundscape as well—the more natural sounds (crickets, birds) and the less car noise, the better. I also manage the scents in my life with essential oil diffusers.

- **Reconnecting to our roots, our inner worthiness, is no small task.** At the same time, tiny steps toward inner integration can make a world of difference. Returning to our innate worthiness can be both the most challenging and the simplest thing we can possibly do. It requires tremendous courage to face inward and set down the armor we've all been taught to live with, and remembering our inherent power can take a little bit of practice. It runs directly up against just about everything the toxic parts of society have been forcing and manipulating us to believe for all this time.

When in doubt, just breathe. Root. And remember.

SOUL SOIL EXERCISES

- Block out some time to go through the "Living a Regenerative Life: Practical Steps" list above and engage in a life assessment. How much of the goodness from this list are you receiving in life, and how much calls out to be integrated? Take out your journal and freewrite for at least ten minutes about what comes up.

- Focus on one of the above categories for a week. Where can you invite more yin, more pleasure in your life? Reflect on how this can help you create a regenerative life.

- Reflect on the idea and practice of living an aligned, regenerative life. Where do you still feel the pull of external validation, the urge to mine or extract energy from yourself and the earth? Reflect on the concept of energy in balance and in flow, in harmony with nature. Freewrite your feelings about this for at least ten minutes.

OUTER WORK

When it comes to outer work, changing our habits about what we buy and eat, our actions in our neighborhoods and cities, our political advocacy and activism, and our degree of support for organizations committed to human rights and healing the soil are all direct ways to impact the world at large. These steps may seem mundane in the face of the massive scale of climate change, but these are the brass tacks of life.

- **Support farmers that take care of the soil.** Vote with your fork. Buy food from small farmers (directly or at farmers' markets) and ask if they practice regenerative agriculture. Talk to the farmers about their soil, and make sure they are taking care of the microbial life and not using synthetic pesticides! You can also get their advice about your own garden. Also, whenever possible, frequent restaurants that support these farmers. Find out where the farmers sell their food, and ask restaurants where they source their food.

- **Every single conversation on these matters contributes to the larger movement.** They signal to food producers that people care what they are eating and are becoming more educated about it. When you can't make it to the farmers' market, buy organic. This does not guarantee that the soil your food has been grown in is healthy, but it raises the odds quite a bit. It also guarantees that no industrial pesticides or herbicides have been used on your food and that you are not eating GMOs (genetically modified organisms). On that note, sell any stock you might have in companies that support or engage in destructive agriculture. If you can, buy stock in companies that are doing it right. As I've been updating this book, the world of regeneratively sourced products has grown immensely and the landscape continues to change year over year. Regenerative labeling is improving, while more and more people are hard at work creating these businesses and products for the economy we all desire.

- **Identify and contact your democratic representatives, and vote.** Wherever you live, let your representatives know that you want to see regenerative agriculture, gender equity, and healing with indigenous peoples prioritized. Functioning and thriving democracies are essential to creating a more regenerative world. Learn about feminist climate justice, an intersectional framework for action through policy and structural change.[3] Follow the QR code in the introduction for up-to-date research, resources, and actions. Call out corruption and participate with your advocacy and activism, and vote!

- **Give to organizations that replenish grasslands, agricultural land, and forests by healing the soil, as well as those that empower women and girls.** If your cup is overflowing, share the wealth. Donate to any organization working for healing grasslands through regenerative herding; protecting and healing forests and regenerating agricultural land; and those dedicated to helping women and girls around the world. Donate time and expertise to these organizations, including posting on social media, messaging and marketing, and contributing however you can to spread the word about the good work they do.

- **Spread the word and encourage others to take these steps.** This matters! Educate yourself by looking at the resources I've provided and beyond. Then educate and enroll your friends, family, colleagues, and strangers in the movement. Are you a social media maven? Get on it! Do you have a blog or a speaking platform? Once you get yourself educated, start shouting it from the rooftops! And you don't need to be a soil scientist or an expert in anything. Just the simple message that the soil is alive and we need to protect it because it is connected to everything is incredibly powerful. Standing up for women and girls and supporting them is also vital to human survival, and the stories you share in this regard can be simple and direct. Own your voice and speak the truth. The most important thing to understand and communicate is that we have mission-critical solutions to the climate emergency that don't require new or expensive technology, which are also no-brainers for food and water security, for community, and for nature at large.

Remember that we are working with Mother Nature at every turn. Each small action makes a difference, and the intention with which we build our regenerative lives is building the new world. Co-create and vote for the world you desire to see with every action. Vote with your fork, but also with your money. Furthermore, vote with your vote! Grow food at home, be mindful whom you buy your food from, be mindful where you eat, support regenerative policies at all levels of government (making calls, spreading the word), vote in elections, and pass it on. Do yoga, meditate, or whatever else serves your inner self. Heal Spirit, earth, and body. Deepening your personal practice and education will fortify everything you say and do. Everything here is extremely doable, and every act in a positive direction makes a huge difference. This is how the tidal wave begins for the world we desire to create.

12

OWNING OUR POWER

Our ability to do our good work in the world depends on our ability to hold our own center. Owning our power is about the inherent power within us. When we own our power, we claim our personal healthy feminine and masculine energies, and learn to recognize and protect ourselves from the toxic feminine and masculine. We heal within ourselves and say no to toxicity and abuse from others. We strengthen our healthy relationship with nature and reject destructive behaviors that cause harm.

Most of us are taught our entire lives that our power is somehow outside of us. That we must earn it and that it's defined by things that society dictates—looks, jobs, money, partners, and so on. Owning our power is about planting our feet on the ground, taking up space, and being fully here. It's about knowing how much power we already hold within our own bodies and our own breath.

This phase of inner and outer works takes courage and commitment. One of the most jarring exercises I had to do during my yoga teacher training was to stand inside a circle of over twenty peers and announce, "I know my value. I honor my healthy boundaries." I stood there for several minutes weeping before I could even choke out the words. I realized that I had never actually practiced healthy boundaries and, furthermore, I had such a limited sense of inherent worthiness that was not externally earned. I had been giving my power away in so many ways up until that point. And just about anyone could take it from me—in my studies, in my work, and in my relationships—because I hadn't the slightest idea that I was already an infinitely perfect expression of the universe exactly as I was. I finally understood that if I thought I could earn my worthiness through work, money, looks, relationships, titles, or whatever, it meant that anyone without those things had to be less worthy than me. It created a trap where either I or the other person was less than. This is how we get into the comparison trap.

When we own our power, we know our inherent worthiness, we are rooted and grounded, and we exercise healthy boundaries. We do not accept manipulation or abuse. We guard and protect ourselves and our loved ones from those who would attempt to extract from us. Rather than self-abandoning, contorting, and people-pleasing, we love who we are and we express as our authentic selves without interference.

BOUNDARIES AND COMMUNICATION

We can't talk about the root chakra and owning our power without talking about boundaries. Boundaries and communication are the bridge between us owning our power and us moving within the world. It's all about speaking our authentic truth and standing in our integrity. Our boundaries are formed by saying *yes* and *no* (and sometimes *maybe*). By our ability to speak our needs and have them honored. These boundaries can be flexible, like personal space, and are not the same thing as having and holding walls between ourselves and others. Healthy boundaries require a connection with the throat chakra and speaking our truth about our bodies, our time, our space, our needs, and our desires.

Originally designed for peacemaking in the 1960s, I've found Marshall Rosenberg's NVC (Nonviolent Communication)[1] to be an incredibly powerful approach. This method offers individuals tools for neutrally communicating their needs, feelings, and desires without emotional manipulation and codependency. It also focuses on taking responsibility for emotions, actions, and choices, while communicating with honesty, empathy, and compassion. Nonviolent Communication is a significant antidote to the blaming, shaming, controlling, and comparing language that fuel destructive forms of relationship. Boundaries and communication are where the rubber meets the road of owning our truth, speaking it, and communicating our needs.

We keep our hearts open while honoring our healthy boundaries by owning our power. We protect our own privacy and integrity. Our lives become our own, and we feel safe to express our authentic self. We are not easily manipulated, coerced, or fed upon energetically. When we own our power, we can better protect ourselves emotionally, psychologically, and spiritually. Our sacred *yes* and our sacred *no* come naturally and intuitively. Nothing needs to be forced. This can definitely be easier said than done. Again, simple but not easy. This can take some adjustment when the standing culture is massively codependent and the tendencies of that culture are mistaken for being normal. Shifting out of these behaviors requires us to untangle and deprogram ourselves from within. Owning our power with healthy boundaries and clear communication creates the solid structure for our feminine, sacral energy to express and play.

PLAY, LIGHTNESS, LAUGHTER, CREATIVITY, AND THE UNEXPECTED

Here, we enter a space where owning our power, communicating well, holding heartfelt boundaries, and incorporating play and creativity all converge. The creative life force of the universe runs through everything, including us and all of nature. Laughter is one of the greatest medicines available to humanity, a healing balm that reminds us of our safety and aliveness.

Clearing out our relational fields, personal and professional, of toxicity and manipulation, gives us considerably more space in our lives to enjoy, create, and expand. The personal work required to heal from the ground up, in the face of the innumerable challenges of being human, can be extremely difficult. Rather than letting it discourage and drain us, I highly recommend sometimes turning to comedy as one option to decompress and remember that lightness is also essential to life.

I also personally love dancing, alone or with others, as a joyful release and expression of the fun in life. Always remember to have fun. Refilling our wells with joy, laughter, movement, and creative expression helps to remind us what we are doing all this work for in the first place. It reminds us what we are fighting for when it comes to restoring that which we feel has been lost or corrupted.

Creative boundaries are also incredibly important, whether that means making private space for play, or protecting a writing, art, or musical project. Creative life force and authentic expression are inherently attractive, and protecting your good vibes is essential to owning your power. The gestational process of many creative works is delicate and private. Allow others to pursue their own creative expression while giving your own the space and time it needs.

The balance of the healthy, fertile, creative feminine and healthy masculine boundaries and drive is expressed beautifully here. There is no space for the toxic feminine and masculine in the precious and sacred experience of play and creativity. The delight of the unexpected also has space to show up when we lean into fun, creative work, and play.

SACRED SEXUALITY: THE CREATIVE LIFE FORCE OF THE UNIVERSE

How do we own our power in an area so tender for most everybody? The sacred sexual can be a place for deep personal reflection and healing, as well as play and pleasure. If there is trauma here, individual work with a trusted professional can guide essential parts of the process. With or without professional support, dropping deep into one's own journey, away from the input of others, can afford the time and space necessary to find one's own experience and truth.

This topic can be particularly tender because of the large amount of spiritual wounding that has occurred and continues to occur from damaging individuals and institutions. These span from elements of organized religion, to the new age, to simply manipulative individuals, with views ranging from purity culture to polyamory. Compound wounding can also occur, when a person leaves a particular ideology only to find themselves entering a different ideology with a similar level of abuse. Here we return again to the toxic feminine and masculine, and forms of abuse range from manipulation to coercion to force, all of which are abjectly unacceptable violations. The energy of control and taking run through all of these, and we return to our power by utilizing our healthy *no* and returning again and again to our own inherent worthiness, integrity, and responsibility.

When we think about the balance of healthy reciprocity, within ourselves or with a partner, the healthy feminine and masculine are in a gorgeous dance of giving and receiving with enthusiasm. Strong, healthy, clear boundaries for ourselves and around any partnership we might be in are essential to giving the sacred sexual a safe space to express with enthusiastic consent. With so many strong and forceful views about sexuality in existence, including high levels of manipulation, it can be challenging to identify people operating with high levels of integrity and responsibility in the sexual healing space. My thoughts on this could fill another volume (and may one day), but I recommend deep work with oneself and internal trauma work with great care about the choice of any practitioner, guide, or person with an interest in affecting your process. Discernment here is key, and is well worth a lifelong practice of strengthening and tending.

Each personal expression of the sacred sexual is different. That's part of the abundant diversity of nature. There's no one size-fits-all answer to what will serve the highest good of any individual. But there's transformative power in self-love and giving ourselves permission, as well as rescinding authority from any entity that wants to lay claim to our bodies, our pleasure, our expression, and our reproductive rights. Our joy, our pleasure, and our bodies belong to us.

BRINGING IT ALL TOGETHER

Owning our power is multifaceted. It involves elements of life that may seem very far from the climate emergency; however, healing from the ground up invites us to reconnect with a wider perspective about what is needed and what is possible. It refocuses us on the art of healthy reciprocity with integrity. It asks us to inquire about many parts of our lives and our journeys that weave together in a great fabric of family, community, society, and ecology. It invites us to ponder the magical nature of the interconnectedness of all things. It urges us to acknowledge rupture and repair, heartbreak and hope.

The dance of the healthy feminine and masculine energies can support us reflecting upon the inherent balance in nature and the universe, and our role within it. The co-creative life force running through us is our birthright to discover and explore. Stopping the toxic feminine and masculine from interfering allows us to protect the sacredness of ourselves, our loved ones, and the beloved earth. Discernment helps us navigate these tricky waters and leads us to safe shores.

Honoring our healthy boundaries; reveling in joy, lightness, laughter, creativity, and the unexpected; and healing within the sacred sexual are all important elements of living a regenerative life. Balance, reciprocity, integrity, and interconnectedness are key ingredients of being in thriving symbiosis with nature. Connecting with a non-sectarian Source energy within ourselves and the great divine mysteries of nature and the universe can remind us that we are not alone and we are always held.

Staying curious about what we do not know, or even what we think we know, can encourage our ongoing growth and learning in this process. Remembering that we are a part of nature, not just affected by it, can help us look to the small and simple within the vastness of creation. With a regenerative mindset, we can reclaim and renew parts of our lives, energy, and choices, which can add up to a more abundant relationship with nature and our spirits.

Rooting down into our inherent worthiness, and remembering the infinite nature of our souls, can help us step into our sense of responsibility and care for all beings. Healing from the ground up can be an incremental, gentle, step-by-step process. We can also experience big breakthroughs; although, like tending to a plant, the fabric of our lives is made up of daily practice. From this space of rooting down, finding our center, and owning our power, everything is possible.

13

WHAT'S POSSIBLE

What's possible is us waking up to the truth of interconnection. What's possible is reconnecting to where our food comes from—worldwide—as well as the healing of our agricultural systems. Doing this can ripple out, heal the economy, and help us with the twin problems of obesity and malnutrition. What's possible is clean drinking water, more biodiversity, and healing our oceans. This will take a good deal of relatively simple action. It doesn't live in the technological future, and it's not at all more than we can afford within our existing economic structure. It's well within our reach and it would be absolute folly to do anything other than to take focused, concerted action starting right now in every way possible to move this train forward. Yes? Yes.

SOUL MEETS SUSTAINABILITY

Let's walk forward together feeling alive, satisfied, enriched, and inspired. Remember, institutions do not lead; they follow. Institutions are just groups of people with sets of agreements. When those agreements fall apart, the institutions fall apart. When we make new agreements, new institutions are formed. Now, people and institutions do tend to be path-dependent, meaning they tend to keep doing whatever they are already doing until something disrupts the path. We are told that institutions are difficult to move and change, and in many ways they are, but we forget that they simply follow the lead of what is demanded of them. Corporations, for example, can only sell what people buy. If we change our minds about what we're going to buy, corporations will unequivocally change what they sell. It has already happened untold times throughout the course of modern history. The global organic food market, for example, was estimated to be valued around USD $228.84 billion in 2024 and continues to grow rapidly along with awareness.[1]

We have no good reason to not work to heal our soil. And we do this by doing it. It's that simple. We bring the future that we want into being by setting a clear intention and then doing it. If you have practiced setting intentions in your own life, you were probably blown away by what you were able to create by simply getting clear on what you wanted to do and then moving forward to execute that intention. The same process works at every level—individual, city, state, national, and international. The Universal Declaration of Human Rights, although still a work in progress, put a stake in the ground for a collective intention and changed the world forever by laying a foundation of agreed-upon values after two catastrophic world wars. The Declaration is still cited and invoked around the world, and it plays an important role in international law. So far, our collective progress has been slowed considerably by extractive and abusive influences baked into our institutions, but we can get a glimmer of what's possible. During World War II, more than 40 percent of all produce came from individual victory gardens, grown by people on their own land—although that time, too, has a dark history of stolen land and Japanese and German internment. We can do better by seeing what's possible through decolonization gardens, climate victory gardens, or regenerative gardens, or whatever we desire.

Growing our own food is healthier, more financially sustainable, more joyful, and way more carbon friendly than purchasing food from other sources. Even growing a few tomato plants and some herbs can brighten our days and give us something nutritious (and nearly free). Also, in the abundant nature of Mother Nature, each tomato yields seeds that we can collect and grow even more plants with; and, as I covered earlier, a number of plants can be regrown in just half an inch of water by keeping their ends. My little indoor basil plant and my outdoor rosemary bush regularly add flavor to my meals. I've also found that simple, hardy plants lend a sense of security and well-being from their steady, nourishing presence. And as if that weren't enough, there are all sorts of indoor plants that will help clean the air in our spaces. Any beginner can start small and learn just about everything they need to get going both online and by asking around.

While I know that the importance of regenerative agriculture is worthy of catching fire, right now it's at a relatively slow burn—but growing. In 2024, 6.8 percent of US adults are aware of regenerative agriculture as a climate, water, and wellness solution, compared to 4 percent in 2023, according to the organization Kiss the Ground.[2] The issues of soil and agriculture made a strong showing at COP21 in Paris, the path-breaking international climate change meeting in early December 2015. The French government's proposal for all countries to increase their soil carbon by 0.4 percent[3] (which would translate to billions of tons of carbon drawn down from the atmosphere if applied worldwide) took hold, and was signed by dozens of countries and organizations. While it flew under the mainstream radar, this agreement marked a major step in the journey to creating actionable steps for governments, farmers, organizations, and individuals around the world. Since then, activities by numerous organizations, businesses, activists, and artists have blossomed, bringing regenerative agriculture increasingly into the academic and policy climate and agriculture discussions, and into mainstream awareness.

THE POWER OF COLLECTIVE INTENTION

One of the biggest takeaways from my PhD dissertation about whether urban sustainability plans affect outcomes is that yes, they do. Plans are essentially collective intentions. They stake a claim, and then to be in integrity, city officials must put their money where their intention is. And in each case that I studied, they did. It's a bit like saying out loud to friends and family when your book draft will be done. The internal intention, backed up by public accountability, opens up the path for the goal to be completed. And when goals are not being met, it shines a light on what might be missing. The other day, a friend of mine sent me one of those inspirational viral memes with a quote by Greg Reid:

> A dream written down with a date becomes a goal.
> A goal broken down into steps becomes a plan.
> A plan backed by action makes your dreams come true.

So for any cynics in the audience who may be sold on the basic premise of healing the soil to balance out the carbon cycle but aren't yet ready to believe it can actually be done, this is the way forward. In order to create anything, somebody must first believe in it and be willing to fight for it. Not only fight for it, but also initiate and take the steps necessary see it through to completion. This is as true in the entrepreneurial world as it is in the policy and artistic worlds. This work of healing the soil is thoroughly divine. And so is every piece of art, every piece of research that moves science forward, every act of advocacy, and so on. All work that involves creating something is creative work. And all creation is divine.

> The great lessons from the true mystics, from the Zen monks . . . is that the sacred is in the ordinary, that it is to be found in one's daily life, in one's neighbors, friends, and family, in one's back yard, and that travel may be a flight from confronting the sacred . . . To be looking elsewhere for miracles is to me a sure sign of ignorance that everything is miraculous.[4]
>
> —ABRAHAM MASLOW

Let's imagine a world in which we have more nutritious food, more food for the world, more clean water, less runoff, healthier ecosystems, and less carbon in our atmospheres and oceans. Healthy soil creates all these things. Rather than zeroing in on the climate crisis, let's instead envision ourselves righting the whole system. It's possible to create what we want on this planet. To put it back into balance, we must only understand the basics and then take action.

Let's imagine a world where we compost instead of using synthetic pesticides and fertilizers. Let's create a world where we understand the importance of fungi and work with them instead of against them. Where women and girls are truly supported and protected. Let's create a vision that is in line with love and connectedness and good food. And then let's execute on that vision. Let's create regenerative lives and a regenerative world. We live in a realm of infinite possibility. We've been doing it wrong for a while now, but that's okay—we can correct our course. It won't happen by accident, though. We actually have to focus on what needs to change and then take the steps to change it. We take care of soil, we take care of ourselves, we take care of each other. We're all one.

This is a clear call to action. There are things every one of us can do today to start to right the system. If we normally go to the supermarket and buy whatever without giving it a second thought, we can instead choose to pay attention to where our food comes from. If it's available and possible, we can buy organic, and support farmers' markets, too. If we have the opportunity to ask our farmers about their soil, we do. And ultimately, we can grow our own food, knowing firsthand where it comes from and saving transport costs and gas.

Growing our own food is an act of revolution. We must get back to our roots. Back to the basics. We must realize limitation in order to transcend it. Dig in. Dig deep. Do the work. And receive. Acknowledge what we're pretending not to know. Our work will require changing our systems from the inside, and it will require changing our lives and ourselves from the inside.

I was talking to a family member one day about American politics, and they passionately pointed out that the people who talk about "making it on their own" seem to have no concept of how much they actually rely on the government—roads and bridges, the military, child labor laws, and the forty-hour work week, just to name a few examples. I took it a step further and reminded them that the government didn't just arbitrarily decide to start working on these things of its own accord; people fought for each of these issues, giving their lives for the cause in a number of instances. They were people like you and me who looked around and decided that the status quo was not good enough. People who decided to do something about it, and to reshape government in such a way that it reflected their values.

Published in 1962, the book *Silent Spring* left a lasting mark on America and the world. In it, Rachel Carson details the dangers of pesticides in poisoning lawns and fields and the bodies of animals and humans. The notion of a silent spring referred to a spring with no robins, as the eggs of robins were emerging too thin to sustain the lives of baby birds, and thus a generation of songbirds were exchanged for a blanket of pesticides in the US. The book invoked the ire of the chemical and pesticide industries, and they relentlessly attacked Carson for being hysterical and ignorant of science. But despite their protests, a chord was struck with the American public—especially with American mothers.

American mothers are, as a cohort, by far the largest food purchasers in the country and in the world. They choose what America eats, they run homeowners' associations, and they vote. If every mother in America decided to make a small set of different choices at the dinner table and diverted some food purchasing to small garden growing, the whole world would change very quickly. And, as happened after *Silent Spring* was published, if these mothers turn their passion to politics, path-breaking laws will be enacted and shit will get done. *Silent Spring* is largely credited as a major instigator in the public awareness and outcry around environmental pollution in the '60s, leading to the National Environmental Policy Act, as well as other far-reaching environmental protections.

Mother Nature is part of our collective psyche. Our internal disconnection is showing up in the physical world. We are facing our own extinction, our own demise, because we have been blind to humanity's deepest truths within us. We desire better than this. We know how to get there. It's in our bones. It's both simple and complex. We are remembering. It requires courage to face the truth—the truth of our connection with nature within ourselves, within our own hearts. The light that can illuminate our inevitable pathway home to balance, harmony, and reciprocity. Breathe. Find your feet. Find your heartbeat. The eternal love guiding us all is available.

SOUL SOIL EXERCISES

- Set some intentions for yourself at the next new moon. Make a list of whatever feels comfortable that you can commit to. This doesn't have to be in goal form—you can intend to breathe more deeply each day or commit to a specific practice.

- Check in with your intentions at the following full moon. Take out your journal and freewrite for at least ten minutes about what comes up. You can also set intentions for longer timeframes as you get comfortable.

- Reflect on aligning your food purchasing, food growing, and political activism. Where could you show up in small ways? Where could you show up in bigger ways? Freewrite your feelings about this for at least ten minutes.

14

THE DIVINE DANCE

The dance of the healthy divine feminine and masculine. Maybe it's what everything's about at the end of the day. Centered and rooted. In flow. The balance and interconnectedness of all things. The beauty of reciprocity, giving and receiving in integrity. Creativity, reciprocity, nurturing, stewardship, guardianship, and responsibility. While so many of us feel great heartbreak about the state of the world, perhaps there is real hope. Perhaps there is a path forward, one that honors our inner balance as well as the greater systems we are all a part of.

Both the inner work and the outer work of facing the climate emergency can feel daunting. Tending to our emotional landscape and mental health requires that we be with our sadness, grief, rage, confusion, and sense of helplessness when they arise. Holding space for others can contribute to the greater process we are all moving through, as an interconnected fabric. Making even small changes in our awareness and daily lives can empower us to take our places as worthy parts of a greater whole.

Regardless of our spiritual background or greater ideologies, connecting with Mother Nature can help us remember the humility in the fact that we all come from the soil, and will all eventually return. We can also rest in the knowledge that when we work with the Earth and her systems, rather than taking and extracting, true abundance flows. An abundance that grows and deepens over time, rather than dwindling or collapsing. Perhaps real "economic growth" is reflected in the abundance of nature, rather than numbers on a page.

We have an opportunity to root down energetically, to build from our foundations and heal from the ground up. To remember our inherent worthiness and let go of the illusion of having to earn our worth. With gentle self-inquiry for our minds, and somatic practices for our bodies and nervous systems, we can learn to move with a yin energy of slowing down, resting to receive. We can question the dominant culture of hierarchy, manipulation, abuse, competition, and burnout. We can remember to breathe.

We also have the opportunity to honor and meet the collective legacy of intergenerational trauma. Real trauma recovery is not easy and can be a lifelong journey. However, freeing ourselves from lines of systemic and individual abuse is perhaps one of the most worthwhile pathways toward a healthier earth. Learning how to become discerning about the toxic feminine and masculine can profoundly strengthen our ability to navigate a challenging world. We have the power to change our systems and institutions—one person, one relationship, one family, one community at a time.

Perhaps, start where you are. Start with the simples. Start with gratitude. A small daily practice can create great benefits over time. Even reflecting on the sacred nature of the land where you are, every cell in your body, and the food you eat can shift the way you balance your life. Practice healthy giving and receiving, honoring healthy boundaries, and connecting with the creative life force within you. Take breaks, unhook from social media, and connect with the physical world. Listen to your body's signals. Breathe.

Perhaps the deep heartbreak of the climate crisis and all the socio-political disasters that humans are both witnessing and creating can point us toward a place for healing within each of us. Maybe a non-sectarian connection to the fabric of the natural universe can help us remember just how valuable we are in the great web of life. Perhaps it can remind us of the value of reciprocal, honorable relationships with each other and all that is. The in-breath and the out-breath can remind us of the life-death-rebirth cycles of nature. My feet on the earth can remind me of belonging, rootedness, worthiness, and foundation. And as my cells regenerate and the divine dance of all things continues, I remember my humble mortality, and I remember the truth of love. Running through all things. Inhabiting every creature. The energetic life force of the universe.

May we all move forward with the following blessing:

May we understand our own deep interconnectedness to all things and honor Mother Nature. May our actions align with the highest good of our inner selves and of all things in the universe. May we bless all food that moves in and out of our bodies so that it may serve the highest good of all. May we bless all money that moves in and out of our lives so that it may serve the highest good of all. May our disagreements serve only to increase understanding, knowledge, and well-being. May we remember our true nature and remember that we are part of nature. May hope replace fear everywhere and lead to all institutions rising to the highest good of all. May truth, peace, and love prevail. And so it is.

ACKNOWLEDGMENTS

To my beautiful partner Jayden John Lee, I love you. Thank you for your immense support in bringing this project to life. Thank you for your music, your art, your integrity, your brilliance, your heart, and your vision. You make everything possible. Thank you for being.

To Mother Nature, The Great Mystery, the plant, animal, and fungi kingdoms.

To my family, immediate and extended. To my grandparents, ancestors, and loved ones on the other side. To Luna, the biggest badass around. To the Lees and the Johns, thank you for your love and support.

To my agent, Amanda, for believing in me, this project, and what's possible for our world. To my editors, Angela, Diana, Rebecca, and Robert, and to Jamie, Jade, Chloe, and the Sounds True team for saying yes to this book and helping me shape it into what it is today.

To all those who supported this book in its earliest stages. A special thanks to Paul and Cheryl J. Marshall for your incredible support. To Micha, for your insight, encouragement, and wisdom.

To my PhD committee, David, Tridib, and Manuel.

To the Kiss the Ground team (past, present, and future) for bringing this story to so many and supporting this writing.

Deep bow to all that is, and the interconnectedness of all things.

NOTES

PREFACE

1 National Oceanic and Atmospheric Administration, "2024 Was the World's Warmest Year on Record," January 10, 2025, noaa.gov/news/2024-was-worlds-warmest-year-on-record.

2 Rebecca Lindsey, "Climate Change: Atmospheric Carbon Dioxide," NOAA Climate.gov, May 21, 2025, climate.gov/news-features/understanding-climate/climate-change-atmospheric-carbon-dioxide.

3 Andrew Moseman, "What Is the Ideal Level of Carbon Dioxide in the Atmosphere for Human Life?," Climate Portal, MIT, May 18, 2021. climate.mit.edu/ask-mit/what-ideal-level-carbon-dioxide-atmosphere-human-life.

4 "Ocean Warming | Vital Signs," NASA, accessed February 12, 2025. climate.nasa.gov/vital-signs/ocean-warming/?intent=121.

5 James R. Riordon, "NASA, NSIDC Scientists Say Arctic Winter Sea Ice at Record Low," NASA, March 27, 2025, nasa.gov/earth/arctic-winter-sea-ice-at-record-low/.

INTRODUCTION

1 Katharine Wilkinson, "How Empowering Women and Girls Can Help Stop Global Warming," filmed November 2018 at TED Women 2018, video, 13:40, ted.com/talks/katharine_wilkinson_how_empowering_women_and_girls_can_help_stop_global_warming.

2 Special thanks to Z. Murdoch for this title and creative concept.

CHAPTER 1: IMAGINE THE YEAR 2050

1 "WMO Confirms 2024 As Warmest Year on Record at About 1.55 °C Above Pre-Industrial Level," World Meteorological Organization, press release, January 10, 2025, wmo.int/news/media-centre/wmo-confirms-2024-warmest-year-record-about-155degc-above-pre-industrial-level.

2 World Meteorological Organization, "WMO Confirms 2024 as Warmest Year on Record."

3 "New Record Daily Global Average Temperature Reached in July 2024," Copernicus Climate Change Service, July 25, 2024, climate.copernicus.eu/new-record-daily-global-average-temperature-reached-july-2024.

4 "Global Temperature | Vital Signs," NASA, accessed February 12, 2025, climate.nasa.gov/vital-signs/global-temperature/?intent=121.

5 "Trends in Atmospheric Carbon Dioxide (CO)," *NOAA Global Monitoring Laboratory*, last modified March 14, 2025, gml.noaa.gov/ccgg/trends/mlo.html.

6 NASA, "Ocean Warming | Vital Signs."

7 Riordon, "Arctic Winter Sea Ice at Record Low."

8 Australian National University, "Climate Extremes in 2024 'Wreaking Havoc' on the Global Water Cycle," January 6, 2025, anu.edu.au/news/all-news/climate

-extremes-in-2024-wreaking-havoc-on-the-global-water-cycle.

9 Douglas Busvine, "Russia and US Eye Joint Arctic Energy Projects After Saudi Talks," Politico, February 18, 2025, politico.eu/article/russia-us-saudi-arctic-energy-rdif-ukraine-russia-capital/.

10 "NOAA-led Researchers Discover Ocean Acidity Is Dissolving Shells of Tiny Snails off the U.S. West Coast," National Oceanic and Atmospheric Administration: US Department of Commerce, April 30, 2014, noaa.gov/noaa-led-researchers-discover-ocean-acidity-dissolving-shells-tiny-snails-us-west-coast; Richard Spinrad and Ian Boyd, "Our Deadened, Carbon-Soaked Seas," *New York Times*, October 15, 2015, nytimes.com/2015/10/16/opinion/our-deadened-carbon-soaked-seas.html?_r=0; "Ocean Acidification," National Oceanic and Atmospheric Administration: US Department of Commerce, last updated February 25, 2025, noaa.gov/education/resource-collections/ocean-coasts/ocean-acidification.

11 Michael E. Mann, "Earth Will Cross the Climate Threshold by 2036," *Scientific American*, April 1, 2014, scientificamerican.com/article/earth-will-cross-the-climate-danger-threshold-by-2036/.

12 Chelsea Harvey, "Climate Change Is Becoming a Top Threat to Biodiversity," *Scientific American*, March 28, 2018, scientificamerican.com/article/climate-change-is-becoming-a-top-threat-to-biodiversity/.

13 *Desertification: The Invisible Frontline*, 2nd ed. (United Nations Convention to Combat Desertification, 2014), unccd.int/sites/default/files/documents/12112014_Invisible%20frontline_ENG.pdf.

14 "As Earth Warms, NASA Targets 'Other Half' of Carbon, Climate Equation," NASA, press release,

November 12, 2015, nasa.gov/press-release/as-earth-warms-nasa-targets-other-half-of-carbon-climate-equation/.

15 NASA, "As Earth Warms, NASA Targets 'Other Half' of Carbon, Climate Equation."

16 Todd Ontl and Lisa Schulte, "Soil Carbon Storage," *Nature Education Knowledge* 3, no. 10 (2012): 35, nature.com/scitable/knowledge/library/soil-carbon-storage-84223790/.

17 Anodea Judith, *Eastern Body, Western Mind: Psychology and the Chakra System as a Path to the Self* (Celestial Arts, 2004).

18 Gerardo Ceballos, Paul Ehrlich, and Rodolfo Dirzo, "Biological Annihilation via the Ongoing Sixth Mass Extinction Signaled by Vertebrate Population Losses and Declines," *Proceedings of the National Academy of Sciences of the United States* 114, no. 30 (July 10, 2017): e6089–e6096, doi.org/10.1073/pnas.1704949114.

19 Lauren Morello, "Phytoplankton Population Drops 40 Percent Since 1950," *Scientific American*, July 29, 2010, scientificamerican.com/article/phytoplankton-population/.

20 David Biello, "400 PPM: Carbon Dioxide in the Atmosphere Reaches Prehistoric Levels," *Scientific American* (via Yahoo News), May 9, 2013, yahoo.com/news/400-ppm-carbon-dioxide-atmosphere-reaches-prehistoric-levels-193000811.html.

21 Mann, "Earth Will Cross the Climate Threshold by 2036."

CHAPTER 2: THE LEGACY LOAD

1 T.F. Stocker et al., eds., "Summary for Policymakers," in *Climate Change 2013: The Physical Science Basis*,

IPCC (Cambridge University Press, 2013), 27, 28, ipcc.ch/site/assets/uploads/2018/02/WG1AR5_SPM_FINAL.pdf.

2 Paul Hawken, *Drawdown: The Most Comprehensive Plan Ever Proposed to Reverse Global Warming* (Penguin Books, 2017).

3 "NOAA-led Researchers Discover Ocean Acidity Is Dissolving Shells of Tiny Snails off the U.S. West Coast," National Oceanic and Atmospheric Administration: US Department of Commerce, April 30, 2014, noaa.gov/noaa-led-researchers-discover-ocean-acidity-dissolving-shells-tiny-snails-us-west-coast.

4 J. E. N. Veron, "Mass Extinctions and Ocean Acidification: Biological Constraints on Geological Dilemmas," *Coral Reefs* 27, no. 3 (September 2008): 459–72, doi.org/10.1007/s00338-008-0381-8.

CHAPTER 3: THE STORY OF ALL THINGS

1 Ron Sender et al., "Revised Estimates for the Number of Human and Bacteria Cells in the Human Body," *PLoS Biology* 14, no. 8 (August 19, 2016): e1002533, ncbi.nlm.nih.gov/pmc/articles/PMC4991899/.

2 Nadia Drake, "This May Be the Oldest Known Sign of Life on Earth," *National Geographic*, March 1, 2017, nationalgeographic.com/news/2017/03/oldest-life-earth-iron-fossils-canada-vents-science/.

3 "Cyanobacteria: Life History and Ecology," UCMP Berkeley, accessed June 2, 2025, ucmp.berkeley.edu/bacteria/cyanolh.html.

4 H. Eswaran et al., "Land Degradation: An Overview," in E.M. Bridges, *Response to Land Degradation* (CRC Press, 2001), https://doi.org/10.1201/9780429187957.

5 Core Writing Team, R.K. Pachauri, and L.A. Meyer, eds., *Climate Change 2014: Synthesis Report* (IPCC, October 2014), ipcc.ch/site/assets/uploads/2018/02/SYR_AR5_FINAL_full.pdf.
6 Anu Khan, "What the Latest IPCC Report Says About Carbon Removal," Carbon180, April 8, 2022, carbon180.org/blog/what-the-latest-ipcc-report-says-about-carbon-removal/.
7 Melissa Gallant, "The Dirt on Soil Carbon," Ecosystem Marketplace, February 27, 2018, ecosystemmarketplace.com/articles/dirt-soil-carbon/.
8 Judith D. Schwartz, *Cows Save the Planet: And Other Improbable Ways of Restoring Soil to Heal the Earth* (Chelsea Green Publishing, 2013), 39.
9 Schwartz, *Cows Save the Planet*, 22.
10 Paul Stamets, ed., *Fantastic Fungi: How Mushrooms Can Heal, Shift Consciousness, and Save the Planet* (Earth Aware Editions, 2019).
11 Khan, "What the Latest IPCC Report Says About Carbon Removal."
12 Bill Bryson, *A Short History of Nearly Everything* (Broadway Books, 2004).
13 Schwartz, *Cows Save the Planet*, 34.
14 Matt Ridley, *Genome: The Autobiography of a Species in 23 Chapters* (Harper Perennial, 2000), 25.
15 Lara Bryant, "Organic Matter Can Improve Your Soil's Water Holding Capacity," NRDC, May 27, 2015, nrdc.org/experts/lara-bryant/organic-matter-can-improve-your-soils-water-holding-capacity.
16 Kiss the Ground Team, "With Deep Gratitude," Kiss the Ground, September 29, 2020, kisstheground.com/with-deep-gratitude/.
17 Tagan Engel, interview by YSE News, "Building a Just Food System: A Q&A with Regenerative

Agriculture Lab Advisor Tagan Engel," Yale School of the Environment, June 27, 2024, environment .yale.edu/news/article/building-just-food-system-qa -regenerative-agriculture-lab-advisor-tagan-engel.

18 Claire Qiu, "Holistic Cattle Farming, Environmental Boons: Students Research Regenerative Agriculture," *Daily Trojan*, May 24, 2023, dailytrojan.com/2023 /05/24/holistic-cattle-farming-environmental-boons -students-research-regenerative-agriculture/.

CHAPTER 5: THE CRY OF THE GREAT MOTHER

1 Richard C. Schwartz, *No Bad Parts: Healing Trauma and Restoring Wholeness with the Internal Family Systems Model* (Sounds True, 2021).

2 Matt Ridley, *Genome: The Autobiography of a Species in 23 Chapters* (Harper Perennial, 2000).

3 Jeff Lieberman, "Science and Spirituality: Jeff Lieberman at TEDxCambridge 2011," TEDx Cambridge, January 19, 2012, YouTube video, 14:24, youtube.com/watch?v=N0--_R6xThs.

4 While I am moved by the message of this book, I do not condone the author's use of the word *Negroid* to describe any of the grandmothers. This term is an unfortunate result of the racist beginnings of the field of anthropology and no longer has a place in acceptable language.

CHAPTER 6: INNER WORK AND OUTER WORK ARE ONE

1 Jack Kerouac, *The Portable Jack Kerouac*, ed. Ann Charters (Viking, 1995).

2 Allison Aubrey, "Forest Bathing: A Retreat to Nature Can Boost Immunity and Mood," NPR, updated March 21, 2025, npr.org/sections/health-shots/2017/07/17

/536676954/forest-bathing-a-retreat-to-nature-can-boost-immunity-and-mood.

3 Stephen Levine with Ann Frederick, *Waking the Tiger: Healing Trauma* (North Atlantic Books, 1997).

CHAPTER 8: WE ARE INHERENTLY WORTHY

1 Richard C. Schwartz, *No Bad Parts: Healing Trauma and Restoring Wholeness with the Internal Family Systems Model* (Sounds True, 2021).

2 Learn more about The Work of Byron Katie at her website, thework.com.

3 Alyssa Nobriga, weekend workshop, January 2018. Learn more at alyssanobriga.com.

4 Richard Rudd, *The Gene Keys: Embracing Your Higher Purpose* (Watkins, 2013).

5 Anodea Judith, *Eastern Body, Western Mind: Psychology and the Chakra System as a Path to the Self* (Celestial Arts, 2004).

CHAPTER 9: REMEMBERING WE ARE NATURE

1 Raju Lal Bhardwaj et al., "An Alarming Decline in the Nutritional Quality of Foods: The Biggest Challenge for Future Generations' Health," *Foods* 13, no. 6 (March 2024): 877, pmc.ncbi.nlm.nih.gov/articles/PMC10969708/.

2 Roddy Sheer and Doug Moss, "Dirt Poor: Have Fruits and Vegetables Become Less Nutritious?," EarthTalk, *Scientific American*, April 27, 2011, scientificamerican.com/article/soil-depletion-and-nutrition-loss/.

3 *Common Ground*, directed by Joshua Tickell and Rebecca Harrell Tickell (Big Picture Ranch, 2023), 1 hour, 41 minutes.

4 "The Gut-Brain Connection," Harvard Health Publishing, Harvard Medical School, July 18, 2023,

health.harvard.edu/diseases-and-conditions/the-gut-brain-connection.

CHAPTER 10: FACING DEATH AND REGENERATION

1 Thanks to J. Hunter for significant contributions to this section.

CHAPTER 11: LIVING A REGENERATIVE LIFE

1 Michael Pollan, *In Defense of Food: An Eater's Manifesto* (Penguin Press, 2008).
2 Selena Simmons-Duffin, "Your Appendix Is Not, In Fact, Useless. This Anatomy Professor Explains," NPR, February 2, 2024, npr.org/sections/health-shots/2024/02/02/1228474984/appendix-function-appendicitis-gut-health.
3 Laura Turquet, Constanza Tabbush, Silke Staab, Loui Williams, and Brianna Howell, *Feminist Climate Justice: A Framework for Action* (UN Women, 2023) unwomen.org/sites/default/files/2023-12/Feminist-climate-justice-A-framework-for-action-en.pdf.

CHAPTER 12: OWNING OUR POWER

1 Marshall B. Rosenberg, *Nonviolent Communication: A Language of Life*, 3rd ed. (PuddleDancer Press, 2015).

CHAPTER 13: WHAT'S POSSIBLE

1 "Organic Food Market Size and Share Analysis—Growth Trends and Forecast Report 2025–2033," Renub Research, accessed June 2, 2025, renub.com/organic-food-market-p.php.
2 "Kiss the Ground 2025 Research Reveals Undeniable Momentum in the Regenerative Movement, Yet a Massive Disconnect Within Our Food System," Kiss the Ground, March 18, 2025, kisstheground.com

/kiss-the-ground-2025-research-reveals-undeniable-momentum-in-the-regenerative-movement-yet-a-massive-disconnect-within-our-food-system/.

3 For more information, visit the International "4 per 1000" Initiative, Soils for Food Security and Climate, https://4p1000.org/?lang=en.

4 Abraham H. Maslow, *Religions, Values, and Peak Experiences*, repr. ed. (Ohio State University Press, 1964).

ABOUT THE AUTHOR

Erin Yu-Juin McMorrow, PhD, earned her doctorate in policy, planning, and development from the University of Southern California, studied political and social thought at the University of Virginia, and served as the director of housing policy with the Los Angeles Coalition to End Hunger and Homelessness. She is also a certified yoga teacher, craniosacral therapist, and creative coach. For more, visit erinmcmorrow.com.

ABOUT SOUNDS TRUE

Sounds True was founded in 1985 by Tami Simon with a clear mission: to disseminate spiritual wisdom. Since starting out as a project with one woman and her tape recorder, we have grown into a multimedia publishing company with a catalog of more than 3,000 titles by some of the leading teachers and visionaries of our time, and an ever-expanding family of beloved customers from across the world.

In more than four decades of evolution, Sounds True has maintained our focus on our overriding purpose and mission: to wake up the world. We offer books, audio programs, online learning experiences, and in-person events to support your personal growth and awakening, and to unlock our greatest human capacities to love and serve.

At SoundsTrue.com you'll find a wealth of resources to enrich your journey, including our weekly *Insights at the Edge* podcast, free downloads, and information about our nonprofit Sounds True Foundation, where we strive to remove financial barriers to the materials we publish through scholarships and donations worldwide.

To learn more, please visit SoundsTrue.com/freegifts or call us toll-free at 800.333.9185.

Together, we can wake up the world.

www.ingramcontent.com/pod-product-compliance
Lightning Source LLC
Chambersburg PA
CBHW020326250826
50388CB00036B/693
* 9 7 8 1 6 4 9 6 3 4 4 0 5 *